COGNITIVE BEHAVIORAL THERAPY

HOW TO BUILD BRAIN STRENGTH AND RESHAPE YOUR LIFE WITH BEHAVIORAL THERAPY

A Guide to Self-Empowerment with CBT, DBT, and ACT

COGNITIVE BEHAVIORAL THERAPY
© Copyright 2018 by Tom Shepherd.
All rights reserved.

This document is geared towards providing exact and reliable information in regards to the topic and issue covered. The publication is sold with the idea that the publisher is not required to render accounting, officially permitted, or otherwise, qualified services. If advice is necessary, legal or professional, a practiced individual in the profession should be ordered.

- From a Declaration of Principles which was accepted and approved equally by a Committee of the American Bar Association and a Committee of Publishers and Associations.

In no way is it legal to reproduce, duplicate, or transmit any part of this document in either electronic means or in printed format. Recording of this publication is strictly prohibited and any storage of this document is not allowed unless with written permission from the publisher. All rights reserved.

The information provided herein is stated to be truthful and consistent, in that any liability, in terms of inattention or otherwise, by any usage or abuse of any policies, processes, or directions contained within is the solitary and utter responsibility of the recipient reader. Under no circumstances will any legal responsibility or blame be held against the publisher for any reparation, damages, or monetary loss due to the information herein, either directly or indirectly.

Respective authors own all copyrights not held by the publisher.

The information herein is offered for informational purposes solely, and is universal as so. The presentation of the information is without contract or any type of guarantee assurance.

The trademarks that are used are without any consent, and the publication of the trademark is without permission or backing by the trademark owner. All trademarks and brands within this book are for clarifying purposes only and are the owned by the owners themselves, not affiliated with this document.

Cognitive Behavioral Therapy

HOW TO BUILD BRAIN STRENGTH AND RESHAPE YOUR LIFE WITH BEHAVIORAL THERAPY

A Guide to Self-Empowerment with CBT, DBT, and ACT

TOM SHEPHERD

TABLE OF CONTENTS

Introduction 5
Chapter 1. How Can Psychotherapy Help You? 8
Chapter 2. Psychotherapy 101 15
Chapter 3. The Truth About Psychotherapy 23
Chapter 4. History: Psychotherapy Through Time 28
Chapter 5. Types Of Psychotherapy 37
Chapter 6. The Third Wave Psychotherapies 40
Chapter 7. CBT, DBT, and ACT 46
Chapter 8. Cognitive Behavioral Therapy (CBT) 52
Chapter 9. CBT and Cognitive Dissonance 62
Chapter 10. Overcoming Negative Thinking and Anxiety with CBT 71
Chapter 11. CBT and Anger Management 84
Chapter 12. How to Overcome Bad Habits through CBT 95
Chapter 13. Mindfulness 101
Chapter 14. Dialectical Behavioral Therapy (DBT) 121
Chapter 15. Emotional Dysregulation 125
Chapter 16. Core DBT Skills 133
Chapter 17. Emotion Regulation 148
Chapter 18. Acceptance and Commitment Therapy (ACT) 153
Chapter 19. The Six Fundamental ACT Processes 161
Conclusion 175

Introduction

There's an alarming trend these days: Psychotherapy is on the decline and medication-only treatment are on the rise.

Between 1998 and 2007, the number of people undergoing psychotherapy remained the same but the number of people who turn to medication has drastically increased (from 44% to 57%). This is according to statistics from the federal Agency for Healthcare Research and Quality.

While medication is certainly useful in many cases, this piece of news is terrible for those suffering from mental health problems primarily because it is an indicator that they are probably not getting all the help they need. Psychotherapy has been proven to be effective, so much so that the American Psychological Association has declared a resolution regarding its effectiveness.

And their claims are backed by numerous studies that have been conducted over a long period of time. Not only that: psychotherapy also helps improve health on a long-term basis and even reduces overall need for health services.

This decline is unfortunate because it signifies that so many people are likely unable to use all the tools available to stay healthy.

Psychotherapy, simply known as talk therapy, has helped millions of people around the world who are suffering from emotional and mental health problems such as depression, anxiety, bipolar disorder, negative thinking, and other concerns that are harmful for a person's well-being. This is one of the few medical treatments that can empower people and realize changes they want to see in their lives.

Psychotherapy can help you:

- Stop harmful habits such as getting into too much debt, using drugs, drinking, and even simple detrimental habits such as hair pulling or nail biting
- Understand why certain things make you worry and what you can do about them
- Develop a plan on how you can cope with problems in life
- Create a dependable, stable routine
- Improve relationships with your family or friends
- Identify things that trigger your anxiety or anger
- Detach your genuine personality from the emotions caused by your health problems
- Understand previous experiences that can be traumatic
- Manage stress
- Overcome insecurities or fears
- Understand your emotional and mental health

If you've read the 1st book and this series -- *Stepping Out of Depression and Anxiety with CBT: A Workbook with Simple Techniques to Retrain Your Brain* -- and did the last exercise mentioned in it, you can take out your journal and check on your notes. The workbook is one of the few books that teach self-treatment for beginners. But if this is your first foray into learning CBT and other psychotherapy techniques on your own, don't worry. This book will be your guide from the very basics to the actual exercises.

CBT, like any other therapeutic approach, has its own of flaws. It's not perfect after all. The good thing is that more developments are being made to CBT to overcome its flaws and improve its overall effectiveness. It's your job now, as a practitioner, to be on the lookout for these developments.

In this second book in our series, you will learn about psychotherapy and its background, as well as the other psychotherapy techniques used alongside CBT – Dialectic Behavioral Therapy (DBT) and Acceptance and Commitment Therapy (ACT).

Everybody deserves help. You deserve help. So go ahead and take a look at what psychotherapy is and the techniques that you can try to take control of your mental health.

Chapter 1.
How Can Psychotherapy Help You?

Contrary to popular belief, psychotherapy is more than just *'talking about your problems'*. It is an effective form of therapy where you can resolve your problems through actionable solutions that are backed by science.

Some techniques in psychotherapy involve a lot of your participation. You will have to keep track of your emotions, maintain a journal to record your thoughts or even take part in social events that have caused you worry in the past.

Through psychotherapy, you can look at things in a much different way or develop new ways to respond to people or events.

Many modern psychotherapy techniques are also designed as simple activities that you can do alone, although in some cases, they are done under the supervision of a professional therapist. The sessions are also concentrated on your life problems, your feelings, and your present thoughts.

Revisiting your past experiences can greatly help in understanding your current situation, but focusing on the present can help you experience the gift of the moment and help you build a better future for yourself and for your loved ones.

When you choose to participate in psychotherapy sessions, you may see your therapist more often during the initial phases of the treatment, and as you move on, you can have reduce the frequency of the appointments. There are even sessions that you can choose to do within the comforts of your own home.

Personal Empowerment through Psychotherapy

Psychotherapy is a form of personal empowerment because it will allow you to obtain the attitude, skills, and knowledge you need to cope with your current situation. Through scientific and personalized sessions, you can transform yourself from being a powerless individual to a person who can control his or her own life.

Psychotherapy takes a multi-dimensional approach to improve the capacity of individuals or groups in making decisions and to transform these decisions into actions that will lead to the preferred results.

Effective psychotherapy techniques can help you make informed decisions so you can improve your life. Resolving mental and emotional health problems will allow you to become a more productive member of the society.

In psychotherapy, the person receives no blame for his or her misery. Instead, the treatment emphasizes the fact that we are responsible for coming up with viable solutions.

Through specific psychotherapy sessions, you can enable yourself to gain influence, authority, and power over yourself. You will be able to:

- Increase your ability to identify and follow your moral compass
- Overcome stigma and increase positive self-perception
- Be involved in the self-activated growth process and subsequent actions to rewire your brain towards success
- Learn important skills to improve yourself
- Develop positive thinking about your ability to allow change to happen
- Learn the ability to become assertive in making your decisions

- Get access to a range of options from which you could effectively make your choices
- Get access to resources and information to guide you in your decisions
- Develop strong decision-making skills

Through psychotherapy, you will be able to obtain all the needed attitude, skills, and knowledge so you can effectively cope with the changing world and the current situation you need to handle.

The Stages of Rewiring Your Brain through Psychotherapy

Rewiring your brain through psychotherapy has six stages: pre-contemplation, contemplation, preparation, action, sustenance, and termination.

1. Pre-Contemplation
In this stage, you may not be aware of your problems or you might still be in the stage of denial. More often than not, you may not want to be seen as damaged or broken. Most people who are at this stage usually wish for other people to change or for circumstances to change as in: "How can I get my husband to love me more so I won't feel so miserable ?" or "I will definitely be happier once I got that high-paying job."

2. Contemplation
People who are in this stage are already aware that they have a problem and they are in the process of ruminating about resolving the problem but not in the immediate time frame.

3. Preparation
Most people who are at this stage already discovered psychotherapy and are already taking action to enable the change they want to see. At this stage, you might have already established a goal with your psychotherapist. At this point, you are already aware that change is up to you, and not dependent on the behavior of the people around you.

4. Action

In this stage, you will be required to take specific steps to change your behavior and thinking patterns through rewiring your brain through specific psychotherapy treatments that you will later learn in this book. Because action may usually bring up the feelings of coercion, failure, guilt, and the temptation to go back to your comfort zone, you really need a lot of support during this stage. Statistics show that at any given period, around 15% of individuals who started psychotherapy sessions are still participating in the action phase.

5. Sustenance

In this stage, you need to work with your therapist so you can consolidate the gains you have achieved and avoid relapse. It is crucial to take note that you have unique experiences. Hence, it is not ideal to assume that a specific approach will work because it has worked for other people. Rather, you need to evaluate yourself if the type of psychotherapy session you have chosen is really helping you with your goals.

6. Termination

Those who have already developed cognitive and coping skills are most likely prepared to function better in life. Through self-empowerment, you are now more equipped to pursue a life that is full of meaning. But be sure to take note that these stages have no specific order and relapse could always happen as part of the process.

The key here is to go at your own pace. While this is referred to as a stage of changes, the process is actually non-linear. Hence, the change could come at any stage, which is just normal.

Whom to Seek for Help

While this book can provide you an overview of specific psychotherapy sessions that you may wish to participate in, it is still ideal to seek professional help. Different types of mental health professionals can provide you psychotherapy intervention.

You may seek professional help from psychiatric nurses (PMHN, APRN), counselors (LCPC, LMFT, MS, MA), social workers (CCSW, LICSW, LCSW, MSW, DSW), psychologists (MS, EdD, PsyD, PhD), and of course psychiatrists (MD).

Regardless of who you want to talk with, it is crucial that you are honest with your thoughts and feelings. That's how you can make real progress. It is best to view your relationship with your professional therapist as a partnership, in which you can work together to resolve your mental health issues.

You must never be ashamed of your condition. You are not alone and you deserve a good life. Millions of people are suffering from pain, sadness, anger, depression, and many of them have found relief and are now living a more dynamic, productive, and empowered life thanks to psychotherapy.

Effective Forms of Psychotherapy

In this book, we will explore the different forms of psychotherapy that are proven effective in addressing common mental and emotional health problems. While there are many psychotherapy techniques that your therapist may prescribe - the most common types are the following:

Cognitive Behavior Therapy (CBT)

This form of psychotherapy is a goal-oriented technique, and it is most effective when you take an active role. For instance, CBT can help you understand core beliefs or automatic thoughts that result in negative emotions. A CBT specialist can help you recognize some of the beliefs and thoughts that don't make sense or completely false and help you change them.

The behavioral aspect of this psychotherapy technique will allow you to achieve a more relaxed mind. Then, you can take the necessary actions so you can move closer to your goals. For example, if you are struggling with depression and you have the tendency to withdraw from life, your psychotherapist may encourage you to spend time with your family or friends or participate in productive hobbies. You might also receive coaching sessions so you can confront people, situations, or things that may cause panic or fear. With practice, you can rewire your brain to influence your behavior.

Dialectical Behavior Therapy (DBT)

DBT is a specific form of CBT. The primary difference between the two is that while CBT focuses on *change*, DBT teaches both *acceptance* and *change*. Also, in addition to individual therapy sessions, DBT teaches behavioral skills through group therapy sessions.

DBT specialists are trained to assure you that your feelings and behavior are understandable and valid. The key tenet in DBT is that you will understand the personal responsibility to change your behavior that is disruptive or not healthy. DBT techniques are designed to constantly remind you when your behavior is disruptive or unhealthy or when you are overstepping a boundary. You will also learn how you can better deal with situations that are similar in the future.

Acceptance and Commitment Therapy (ACT)

ACT is a special form of DBT that is focused on the problem of human suffering. ACT specialists will guide you in understanding human suffering as an important factor in realizing a good life. This new form of CBT is focused on important questions such as "What is my real purpose in life?"

As you go along with this book, try to understand the merits of psychotherapy and how it can help you. This guide provides you a comprehensive overview of the available forms of psychotherapy that could help you overcome your mental and emotional health problems such as depression or anxiety disorder.

While you may do the exercises and techniques described in this book, it is still best to work with a professional psychotherapist who can act as your partner in your journey towards living a better life.

Chapter 2.
Psychotherapy 101

Have you ever felt unnaturally overwhelmed with your problems that you can't seem to deal with them, let alone face them? If so, you're not alone.

Many people in the U.S. struggle to cope with stopping from smoking, losing weight, or managing a serious illness. Still, others need help with substance abuse, stress, the death of a loved one, job loss, relationship troubles, or other issues.

Often, these problems can become devastating, unbearable, and even debilitating. At worse, it can cause sufferers to feel incapacitated.

When a person feels this way, it is a clear sign of depression, anxiety, or other mental disorders. In the U.S., the National Institute of Mental Health (NIMH) declared that 1 out of 4 American adults experience mental disorders, the more common of which is depression and anxiety, in any given year.

What Is Psychotherapy?

Majority of terms and distinctions in the world of psychology and psychiatry are blurred with time. It's daunting to understand the multiple meanings of certain words. It is easy to confuse psychoanalysis with psychotherapy, psychologists with psychiatrists, and the many other related terminologies used by those who seek to treat mental health problems or study the mind today. For this reason and before we proceed, let us clarify the definitions of specific keywords we'll discuss throughout the book. With that said, let's learn what exactly psychotherapy is.

Psychotherapy is applied to treat mental disorders, like depression or anxiety. Also called the *talk therapy*, it is a way of helping people with a wide variety of emotional difficulties and mental illnesses. It tackles problems that include difficulties in the death of a loved one, medical illness or loss, the impact of trauma, and basically coping with daily life. It helps control or eliminate troubling symptoms to enable a person to function better, increasing healing and well-being.

To enable people to develop more effective, healthier habits, scientifically validated procedures are used in psychotherapy sessions. Each session provides a supportive, collaborative environment that fosters relationship between a patient and therapist.

This allows the patient to talk openly with nonjudgmental, neutral, and objective, psychotherapist. And because an entire session is grounded in dialogue, both patient and psychotherapist can work together to identify and ultimately change the debilitating patterns in behavior and thoughts.

Aside from solving mental and emotional problems, talk therapy can teach patients new skills to better cope with life challenges by the time treatment is done. This ensures that sufferers know what to do when similar problems arise in the future. Through psychotherapy, sufferers live more productive, healthier, and happier lives.

When considering psychotherapy, you can choose from several approaches including the increasingly popular, cognitive-behavioral therapy. However, some types may only work better with certain issues or problems. It can also be used in combination with other therapies or medication.

The Psychotherapist

A number of different types of health professionals can provide psychotherapy. This includes psychiatric nurses, licensed family and marriage therapists, licensed professional counselors, licensed social workers, psychologists, psychiatrists, and others with specialized training in psychotherapy. Among all of these professionals however, only psychiatrists are trained in medicine and are therefore, able to prescribe medications.

It's important to find a psychotherapist with whom you can work well. You can check out several referral sources including workplace Employee Assistance Programs (EAP), community health centers, medical schools, local psychiatric societies, primary care physicians, and numerous online resources.

In the U.S., federal law requires health insurance to cover mental health services, including psychotherapy, similar to other medical care costs.

Psychotherapy And Medication

At times, psychotherapy is combined with medication to treat mental health issues. However, there are circumstances when only psychotherapy is the best option while medication may be clearly useful in others. Still, there are some that neither psychotherapy nor medication alone is better.

To make the best out of psychotherapy treatment, adequate sleep, regular exercise, good nutrition, and other healthy lifestyle improvements can be important in supporting recovery and overall wellness.

Does Psychotherapy Work?

According to data collected by the American Psychiatric Association, psychotherapy has been linked with positive changes not only in the body, but in the brain as well. It has also been shown to improve behaviors and emotions. Additional benefits include increased work satisfaction, fewer medical problems, less disability, and fewer sick days.

The APA also stated that research on psychotherapy has shown evidence wherein people suffering from certain mental health problems experienced symptom relief after treatment. It enabled sufferers to function better in their lives.

Researchers have been able to determine the positive effects of psychotherapy in patients by using brain imaging techniques. Aside from this, numerous studies from Harvard and the NIMH have identified the result of undergoing psychotherapy as the reason for the brain changes in people with mental illness.

Meanwhile, Hasse Karlsson, chief psychiatrist at Turku University Hospital in Finland and author of *How Psychotherapy Changes the Brain*, mentioned in Psychiatric Times that often, the brain changes caused by psychotherapy were similar to changes caused by medication. However, the American Psychiatric Association advised that to get the most out of psychotherapy, you must follow your treatment plan, approach the therapy as a collaborative effort, and be open and honest. Follow through with any assignments, as much as possible especially between sessions, such as journal writing.

The American mental health crisis that started in the 1950s has caused psychotherapy to take on a new form. The therapy's transformation removed itself from the unchallenged ideas of Sigmund Freud and his contemporary, the Swiss psychiatrist and psychoanalyst Carl Jung.

Back then, when Freud and Jung dominated the scene, psychotherapists toyed with ideas that bordered on philosophy and religion. They used words that faintly suggested a divine power as the source of their understanding of mental health problems. Therapists were then viewed as transcendent beings, creatures to be revered. Thankfully, this has changed since.

Therapists today are warm, lighthearted, friendly, sympathetic, and caring – the outcome of the necessities of unhappy people. To understand how psychotherapy has become a sort of source of necessary artificial friendship, we must look at the various studies conducted over the last six decades about the effectiveness of the talk therapy. In fact, it is another reason why the treatment has been accepted widely in the US. It's because it works.

According to the American Psychological Association, research has revealed that 75% of patients who received psychotherapy has benefited from the therapy. As we discussed in the first chapter, people suffering from mental health problems experience less symptoms, enabling them to function well in their lives.

Psychotherapy has been linked with positive changes in the brain and body, improving emotions and behaviors. It enables sufferers to experience fewer sick days and medical problems, less disability, and all the while, increase satisfaction for accomplished tasks at home and at work.

Researchers have discovered that changes occur in the brain of a person who has undergone psychotherapy. Using of brain imaging techniques, they've found out that people with mental issues including PTSD, panic disorder, depression, and other conditions, experience changes in their brains due to psychotherapy. Surprisingly though, these changes were similar to the effects of prescription drugs for mental problems mentioned earlier.

While there have been many studies done on psychotherapy, its effects are noted in recent research. Here are five studies conducted over the course of a decade that sought to learn more about the effectiveness of psychotherapy:

1. According to a study (Evidence-Based Treatments for Children and Adolescents: An Updated Review of Indicators of Efficacy and Effectiveness) published in the Clinical Psychology: Science and Practice Journal in 2011, the general effects of psychotherapy are significant enough to be widely accepted as an effective treatment for mental health problems. Previous studies from 2001 (The Great Psychotherapy Debate: Model, Methods, and Findings by Bruce Wampold) and 2009 (Making Science Matter in Clinical Practice: Redefining Psychotherapy by Larry Beutler) have already revealed the effects of the therapy were constant although the mental conditions of the patients varied. Where there were differences, they were caused the factors including social support, complexity and intensity of personality, and chronic nature of the mental health problem.

2. Two separate studies from 2006 (Enduring Effects for Cognitive Behavior Therapy in the Treatment of Depression and Anxiety by Hollon, S.D., Stewart, M.O., and Strunk, D.) and 2010 (The Efficacy of Psychodynamic Psychotherapy by Jonathan Shedler) discovered that psychotherapy lasts longer than psychopharmacological treatments. The studies also found out that patients will less likely require follow-up or additional treatments after finishing full sessions of psychotherapy. According to Clinical Associate Professor of Psychiatry at the University of Colorado's School of Medicine, Jonathan Shedler, patients tend to improve after the termination of treatment because of the variety of skills that the therapy teaches.

3. Evidence from rigorous clinical research about most psychological disorders has shown that many forms of psychotherapy are effective not only for the elderly and general adults, but also with children. Along with these studies, done between 2001 and 2010, scientists including Shedler, discovered that the benefits of psychotherapy was far greater than receiving no treatment.

4. This discovery was important because it opened up ways on how different forms of psychotherapy can be improved. Enhancing therapies can help clinical psychologists to customize their treatments according to the needs of their patients.

5. Various researches in 2008 (Adult psychotherapy in the real world by Minami, T., & Wampold, B.E.) and 2009 (Can Treatment Trial Samples Be Representative? by Wales, J.A., Palmer, R.L., and Fairburn, C.G.) established that psychotherapy is generally as effective in routine care and clinical trials.

6. When compared, there is relatively no significant difference in the different forms of psychotherapy. This was according to various studies published in the Journal of Mental Health (2007) and the books Principles of Therapeutic Change That Work (2006) and Psychotherapy Relationships That Work (2011).

Therapy Sessions

There is a need for active involvement between patient and therapist in a psychotherapy session. The trust and relationship between you and your therapist is crucial to working together effectively in which you will benefit from.

However, as with any other medical treatments, confidentiality is a basic requirement in psychotherapy. In addition, while patients share personal thoughts and feelings, intimate physical contact with a therapist is never or useful, appropriate, nor acceptable.

A session, which is mostly 30 to 50 minutes long, may be conducted in an individual, couple, group, or family setting. It's suitable even for children.

Whichever the setting is however, there is a joint planning involved between you and your therapist as to the arrangement, frequency, duration, and goal of your treatment. An entire treatment can range from a few sessions to as long as months or years. Short-term treatments are applied with immediate issues, while long-term treatments are used to deal with complex, longstanding issues.

Knowing the background of psychotherapy will make it easier for you to understand the treatments that will be discussed later in this book. So far, we've tackled some of the basic information about psychotherapy. However, we will also discuss why it is no longer as popular even though it's been in practice since the 1940s.

Chapter 3.
The Truth About Psychotherapy

According to a New York Times 2008 report, there is a decline in the use of psychotherapy as a treatment for mental health problems in the US. We will take a look at the possible reasons and factors. Let's find out.

In The United States

In the US, Sigmund Freud's theories on psychoanalysis were widely accepted. It dominated the world of mental health, encompassing neurology, psychiatry, and psychology. However, post-World War II America forced the discipline of the founder of psychoanalysis to evolve. From his actual practice of therapy, it transformed into a treatment method that was supposedly practical, accessible, and affordable, according to demands of the time.

Military induction centers discovered that many of the Americans signing up for service were not at all fit for service. Soldiers who returned from war on the other hand, were traumatized beyond repair. Families who welcomed their "damaged" sons and daughters sought for immediate relief, and not the long-term self-discovery that were prescribed.

The structure and high cost of psychoanalysis didn't help. In addition, there were not enough qualified psychiatrists who are competent to make use Freud's theories. There was an evidently desperate need for practitioners.

While struggling to meet the need, psychiatrists inadvertently increased the general public's awareness of the talk therapy. It was believed that mere, but intimate, talking with someone who has received some kind of specialized training can help solve and treat mental problems. Based on the people's observation at the time, it was true and effective.

Meanwhile, mental health professionals turned to the problem in response to the demand for the new form of talk therapy and its growing public acceptance. There was a growing similarity with their actual work with clients despite having different roots.

Social workers expanded their practice by working on the personal and interpersonal problems of their clients. Psychologists who previously focused on research and quantification practiced the therapy as well. Psychiatrists minimized their dependency on Freud's theories to guide their work.

Social workers, psychologists, and psychiatrists however, had to work harder to specifically indicate the structure of their therapy sessions and define their profession. While the demand for talk therapy had an impact on the general public, it too had an effect on the work of mental health professionals. It created a competition for the legitimacy of their professions.

Psychologists and social workers performed therapies that were shorter and more targeted. Psychiatrists on the other hand, preferred long-term analysis. With the rise of psychotherapy, the medically-trained psychiatrists' focus shifted. They turned more to psychopharmacology, the study of the effects of drugs on human behavior, thinking, sensation, and mood.

Nothing is more reflective of this, although far wide in between since the need arose decades ago, than what's been currently studied of the trends in outpatient psychotherapy in the United States.

Trends in outpatient psychotherapy in the US were examined in a 2010 study by psychiatrists and psychiatry professors, doctors Steven Marcus (University of Pennsylvania) and Mark Olfson (Columbia University). Their research, originally published in the American Journal of Psychiatry, was featured in a 2010 November article, *Where Has All the Psychotherapy Gone?* on the *Monitor on Psychology* magazine.

Marcus and Olfson's research drew data from a survey conducted by the US Department of Health and Human Services' Agency for Healthcare Research and Quality from years 1998 to 2007.

The doctors discovered that within that decade, the number of the general population who use psychotherapy has barely changed. However, a shift in the outpatient mental health care has occurred within the given time frame.

Over the same period, there was a drop in the use of psychotherapy as a sole treatment and when it was used in combination with prescription drugs. Patients who received psychotherapy treatments dropped to 10.5% from 16%; while those who received medications along with their treatments dropped to 32% from 40%.

On the other hand, the number of patients who went for medication-only treatments, avoiding the psychotherapy part of their overall treatment, increased. With only 44% previously, there were more than 57% patients who relied on just their medications before the decade ended. According to Suzanne Bennett Johnson, former president of the American Psychological Association, insurance providers have played a major role in this resulting situation.

In the US, marketing and advertising have paid off immensely for pharmaceutical companies. They reaped the rewards of aggressively marketing their products to mental health patients. However, this is not the only reason why more and more people who need proper mental health care are acquiring medication-only treatments.

As Johnson pointed out in a 2011 interview with Monitor on Psychology magazine, insurance coverage has included mental health drugs in the bills that they pay for, but not for actual mental health care. She also observed that patients, as forced by habit, would go see their primary-care physician first when symptoms are initially felt or when something about their health bothers them.

Unfortunately, most primary-care providers would rather prescribe drugs than psychotherapy treatments. Johnson added that doctors find it more convenient to write prescriptions than search and recommend mental health care providers that can offer a wide range of treatments. Katherine Nordal, APA's Practice Directorate executive director, on the other hand, expressed her concern for this kind of practice.

Nordal stated that it's alarming to know that people could've been helped well by psychotherapy treatments considering its effectiveness in mental health problems. She also believes that mental health sufferers want a quick fix and thus, prefer medications only.

Still, for the American general public, all this information doesn't lessen the fact that psychotherapy, in all its form, is effective.

In The United Kingdom

The British general public on the other hand, has a slightly different situation going on. While it is perceived that Americans love their *shrink*, the British apparently, love their therapists even more. The profession is growing, particularly for therapists in cognitive behavior therapy (CBT).

Nearly half of all therapy courses in the UK are now CBT. According to a 2014 report by the London weekly newspaper, The Economist, that's 43% of all therapy courses and it keeps on growing. In fact, seven years before the report was released, there were already 6,000 CBT students.

The sudden rise in CBT students and practitioners was a result of its declaration as a standard treatment. According to government research, the deciding factors for adopting CBT as a standard treatment were its effectiveness, faster turn-around, and ability to increase employment rates.

The therapy, although relatively new, has provided a strong body of evidence that it is effective. It also enabled employees suffering from psychological problems to get back on their feet and work again, increasing the country's employment rate. In addition, it produces result quickly. Patients see significant improvement even after just 10 sessions.

The British government has gotten a lot more from adopting CBT as a standard treatment. The therapy expanded the therapy industry, increasing mental health spending from 3% to 7%. In the US however, we've seen the opposite when we discussed the scenario over there earlier. While an increasing number of Americans prefers to take medicine for their depression and anxiety, the British people wanted the actual therapy.

With that said, why do many British turn to talk therapy – something that they're not so familiar about anyway? A valuable reason would be CBT's ability to teach people suffering from mental health issues, especially depression and anxiety, to avoid or work their way around bad, unhelpful, obstructive thoughts. It's more than just talking about your childhood with your therapist.

Aside from this, psychotherapy is much affordable compared to psychoanalysis. Because it's a standard treatment, it has been allotted with public funding. A National Health Service (NHS) program has been provided with £213 million speed up the process of delivering CBT to the public. Other forms of therapy received a budget of £172 million only.

The CBT industry's budget has also enabled it to reach more patients. Patients on the other hand, find it easier to seek a CBT therapist. Hospital departments and general practitioners can now refer free CBT treatments, nationwide.

Perhaps the Americans could learn something from the British people? To understand the so-called decline of psychotherapy in the US, it's crucial to look at its modern history.

Chapter 4.
History: Psychotherapy Through Time

Before the 1950s, psychotherapists were highly regarded for their knowledge of the human mind and emotion. They speak with such authority, providing nearly incomprehensible psychology-talk, that the average Americans were in a way, both amazed and wary of them. That's why seeing a shrink was a taboo then, and now.

However, a lot has changed since then. Today, psychotherapists are a friendly figure. In their new role, psychotherapists provide a form of modern professional care that can serve as a substitute for companionship.

Ronald Dworkin, a senior fellow at the Hudson Institute and author of *Artificial Happiness: The Dark Side of the New Happy Class,* calls it *artificial friendship.*

It's a lonely age after all, with technology occupying most of people's time and energy. Lonely people look to their therapist for some serious interaction, talk time.

The Root Of Conflict

Ever since Freud visited the US in 1909, the American people have been fascinated with psychoanalysis. Despite this, only a tiny fraction of the US population was undergoing some form of psychoanalysis, psychotherapy in particular, by the 1940s.

Unfortunately, the wide fascination over psychotherapy coupled with only a few patients of psychoanalysis, led to many Americans thinking that both are the same. There was also a struggle as to who should practice psychotherapy and who was allowed to treat patients with psychoanalysis.

Psychiatrists are trained in anatomy and biology. Like other medical doctors, they are allowed to prescribe drugs. Most of them worked as superintendents in state mental hospitals during the early twentieth century, which is often depicted in movies.

However, because psychiatrists are medically trained, they have a biological view of mental health problems and illnesses. This meant that they are better at providing psychoanalysis, which was the case in the 1940s when there was a thriving private practice. By 1953, 82% of psychoanalysts in the US were psychiatrists.

The US government however, had something else on its mind. It wanted to provide government support to psychoanalysis and psychotherapy. As a result, it organized a concerted effort to allow non-medically trained psychoanalysts to practice. This threatened both biology-minded and psychoanalysis-focused psychiatrists.

The decision coincided with the fact that the number of medically-trained psychiatrists was not enough to meet the demand. To provide sufficient government support, more non-medically-trained therapists were needed. Now enter the psychologists.

Psychologists are not medically trained, but they obtain an advanced degree. With a graduate training in psychology, majority of psychologists became scientists, working initially in college and university laboratories. They were dubbed as the *academic psychologists*. Treating people using psychotherapy or psychoanalysis was the last thing on their minds.

However, there were a few who practiced their psychology training with patients. *Clinical psychologists* worked with and assisted psychiatrists, often performing tests on patients. Diagnosis and actual treatments were left in the hands of the psychiatrists.

Unfortunately, the difference between the two focuses of psychology caused a rift. Academic psychologists believed those who received scientific method and education in the finest schools are the only ones who deserved to be called real psychologists. Clinical psychologists on the other hand, were idealists. They wanted to pursue Freud's theories and practice psychotherapy.

All the while, a mental health crisis was disabling soldiers who served in World War II and the rest of the country as the effects of war affected many. Patients admitted to outpatient psychiatric clinics and hospitals for mental health problems climbed rapidly. To deal with the problem, the nation only had a few thousand clinical psychologists. There were simply not enough trained mental health professionals.

In 1946, the government responded by creating the National Mental Health Act (NMHA). A few years later, it led to the establishment of the National Institute of Mental Health (NIMH). One of its policies was to provide funds to send more psychotherapists to school.

While both the NMHA and the NIMH attempted to handle the crisis, it inadvertently brought to the surface divisions within the mental health community. Finally, clinical psychologists had the opportunity to train as psychotherapists and practice it without supervision or restriction. They were in fact, the only group that benefited more from the government's new policy on mental health.

In a way, the NMHA caused a conflict between psychiatrists and clinical psychologists in the US. Nine percent of clinical psychologists had their own treatment clinics by the early 1950s. Psychiatrists and academic psychologists on the other hand, fought back. Academic psychologists argued that psychotherapy was unscientific, while psychiatrists maintained that clinical psychologists can't diagnose mental illness.

To defend their ideologists, clinical psychologists began popularizing psychotherapy. Regular psychological columns started to appear on major newspapers. Lifestyle magazines also featured their own psychological sections. The major breakthrough for clinical psychologists was when Cornell University Ph.D. graduate, Joyce Brothers, hosted the first television show that tackled emotional and psychological problems in 1958.

As the awareness for psychotherapy unfolded, psychoanalysis entered the public consciousness. The mental health crisis made people sensitive to topics about emotions and psychological ideas. Freud's ideas were often mentioned by clinical psychologists in their writings, interviews, speeches, and conversations. The public absorbed these ideas, often identifying with their personal concerns. In other words, the American public and clinical psychologists were in sync.

On the other hand, while academic psychologists and psychiatrists were disturbed because of this event, they were powerless against the growth of clinical psychology. People who sought a solution to their mental and emotional problems saw clinical psychologists as the perfect alternative to seeking help from a psychiatrist.

Unfortunately, considering psychotherapy by clinical psychologists was fairly new, it wasn't able to firmly set its position as the best answer to people's mental health problems. It wasn't, at the time, able to solve people's problems. Instead, it only explained why certain mental and emotional issues were occurring. Therapy sessions weren't producing favorable results as well. Even established clinical psychologists expressed their doubts about the effectiveness of early psychotherapy.

This doubt and unstable results started the love-hate relationship of the general public with psychotherapy.

Enter Short-Term Psychotherapy

The mental health crisis of the 1950s didn't stop there. It dragged on into the 1960s.

Social activists blamed psychotherapy for popular support for capitalism. They believed that clinical psychologists were brainwashing and convincing patients, who were mostly middle class, to support the government, follow its capitalist views, and merge it with their values.

Moreover, the social stigma of seeking help for emotional or mental health problems started to emerge. People began feeling conscious of what others will have to say upon learning about their visits to the clinical psychologist. Seeking the help of a doctor seemed to suggest that they were mentally ill and needed to be institutionalized. As a result, clinical psychologists received the derogatory term of *shrinks*, short for head shrinkers, from anxious patients and critics.

The government on the other hand, aimed to deinstitutionalize mentally ill people. President John F. Kennedy signed the Community Mental Health Act (CMHA) into law in 1963. It sought to return people from mental health institutions into the community. Seeking the help of a psychiatrist or clinical psychologists simply for anxiety, depression, and other everyday life emotional problems shouldn't require being locked up in a mental health facility cell.

Although the CMHA helped establish the wider practice of a variety of therapeutic models including psychoanalytic, humanistic, behavioral, and cognitive therapies, it created a new demand for more mental health professionals. Counselors and social workers working in mental health were tapped to fill the gap in community mental health centers that were brought up all over the country.

The establishment of community mental health centers was life-changing for many Americans experiencing unhappiness on a daily basis. They finally had place to go to and ask for help. It also introduced them to psychotherapy.

Mental health professionals however, had to modify their therapy based on what kind of treatment their patients demanded for. Whereas patients from the 1950s simply followed and listened to doctors' orders, mental health sufferers from the 1960s were smarter. Mental health professionals observed how patients made their demands obvious. No longer satisfied with explanations of how their illnesses were acquired or developed, patients want their problems solved – quickly at that.

Patients' demands were time-ordained. The on-going mental health crisis and the demand for a quick solution to mental health problems forced mental health professionals to adapt, thus the birth of short-term psychotherapy.

With just twenty sessions or less, mental health professionals can now attend to as many patients, including walk-ins, as they can in a day. Patients on the other hand saw their therapists as confidantes.

The Revolutionary Solution

In the 1950s, mental health professionals and scientists observed that the average American's major source of worries in life was public opinion. It mattered a lot to people, causing them anxiety beyond manageable.

Twenty years later, people's unhappiness came from their feeling of loneliness. The mental health crisis has indeed, entered a new phase. Psychology Today, a popular psychology magazine at the time (and even today), proclaimed the 1970s as the beginning of the new Age of Depression.

The decade produced some of the most tense and agitated generation in the history of the US, but it also gave birth to the loneliest people of post-war America. It made the effects of depression look even worse than it already was.

Primary care doctors seemingly added to the problem. To them, what the American public was experiencing was caused by chemical imbalance in the brain, which can be cured by prescribed medications. Even without proof, the people bought the idea.

Psychiatrists on the other hand, nearly gave up on their quest to discredit clinical psychologists. They were almost convinced that psychotherapy is doomed. However, when the trend of using drugs to alleviate symptoms of anxiety, depression, and mental health problems in general, started and eventually made profits, psychiatrists saw an opportunity.

Psychiatrists became less concerned with the threat of other mental health professionals to their career and industry. Instead, they aimed to focus on prescribing drugs, which other mental health professionals can't do, and in the process, explore psychopharmacology.

In other words, the 1970s sought drugs as a solution to the country's ongoing mental health problem. It was the decade that saw the joined forces of psychoactive drugs and psychotherapy.

Clinical psychologists had to step back and look at the whole scenario. Primary care doctors and psychiatrists were prescribing drugs to patients while providing philosophical and medical justification for their prescriptions. As some psychologists actively fought the drug trend, the majority realized a need for a more personal, intimate reconnection with patients. They can't prescribe drug, but they can improve and customize the talk therapy.

While primary care doctors pushed their idea that mental illness is rooted in problematic neurotransmitters, psychotherapists offered their own ideas. It was their way of improving the talk therapy in a way that would dismiss the public's doubts and anxieties about the treatment. It was also aimed at changing the image of psychotherapy.

First, clinical psychologists had to ease, if not remove, a person's fear of *shrinks*. The stigma that previous decades started was still being felt in the 70s. From there, they had to detach from the scientist-therapist label, put the need for mental health care through therapeutic conversations, and become a warm, caring friend to their patients.

With these goals in mind, clinical psychologists wanted to treat people suffering from mental health problems by providing them help on how they can find the meaning and nature of human happiness.

To reach their goals, psychologists sought universities to create non-university-based psychology degree programs that would focus more on human behavior than research. As mentioned earlier, psychologists are not medically trained, but their advanced degree enables them to work in research and eventually become scientists. With the newly-created programs, would-be psychologists could receive professional, clinical training.

The first of the new programs was launched in 1969 in the California School of Professional Psychology. The programs produced twice as many clinical psychologists as doctors of psychology for the next 30 years.

A Farewell To Freud's Theories

Other mental health professionals worked together with clinical psychologists to promote the changing image of therapists to that of the caring professional, instead of the disinterested scientists. They presented themselves as *caregivers* who were eager to listen to patients about their everyday life and problems.

A key part of this shift was leaving behind Freud's psychology, which often used terms that were not spoken in everyday language. Clinical psychologists used a simpler vocabulary to explain to average people about what they're going through and connect with them. Americans were finally seeing caring professionals, rather than going to shrinks.

For the years to follow since the mental health crisis of the 1950s, the likes of managed care such as HMOs (health maintenance organizations), PPOs (preferred provider organizations), and IPAs (independent practice associations or independent physicians), helped turned short-term psychotherapy into a new industry as we know it today. The rise of depression, anxiety, loneliness, and other mental health problems has made psychotherapy the preferred remedy.

Chapter 5.
Types Of Psychotherapy

We've learned that research has shown that all forms of psychotherapy produce beneficial results to its recipients. In general, psychologists use one or more theories of psychotherapy with each one providing a roadmap that will guide therapists on how they can better understand the problems of their patients and develop a corresponding solution.

According to the Encyclopedia of Psychology (2000), different forms of psychotherapy are generally divided into five categories:

Humanistic Therapy

Humanistic therapy is influenced by humanistic philosophers Søren Kierkegaard, Martin Buber, and Jean-Paul Sartre. Important themes include respect and concern for others, highlight a person's capacity to make rational decisions, and develop their potential to the fullest. Particularly influential types of humanistic therapy are:

1. Gestalt therapy. It emphasizes the importance accepting responsibility and for being aware of the present. This idea is called *organismic holism*.
2. Existential therapy focuses on the search for meaning, self-determination, and free will.
3. Client-centered therapy helps patients change their outlook in life by emphasizing their own interests, cares, concerns, and inner experiences. It rejects the idea of therapists as authorities.

Holistic or Integrative Therapy

Holistic or integrative therapy puts together different forms of psychotherapies to provide the best possible solutions to patient's mental and emotional health problems. Therapists who practice this approach blend elements to fit patients' needs.

Psychoanalysis and Psychodynamic Therapies

Psychoanalytical therapies are distinguished by the partnership between therapist and patient – they work together in order to resolve issues. It is through this therapeutic relationship that patients are able to learn about themselves. The interactions enable them to explore their thoughts and minds.

Psychoanalysis, being developed by Freud, is closely identified with him. However, its formulations has since been modified and extended.

Traditional psychoanalysis is still practiced today, but it takes on new dynamic forms, thus psychodynamic in nature. These therapies focus on encouraging patients to discover their unconscious motivations resulting in a change in their thoughts, feelings, and problematic behaviors.

Behavior Therapy

Behavior therapy focuses on the role of learning in helping patients develop normal and abnormal behaviors.

Russian physiologist Ivan Pavlov discovered associative learning or classical conditioning, which is an important contribution to behavior therapy. Through his discovery, he observed how his dogs would drool whenever they hear the sound of any bell. It turned out that his dogs has been conditioned to respond to the sound of a bell whenever they were fed. They learned to associate the sound with food, thus their drooling.

Another form of classical conditioning is *desensitizing*. A person with a phobia will be treated by repeated exposure to the person's source of fear or anxiety.

Another type of learning, called operant conditioning, uses rewards and punishments to affect a person's behavior. It was discovered by Edward Thorndike, an American psychologist who helped laid the foundation for educational psychology.

Since the emergence of behavior therapy in the 1950s, it has been developed into several variations. One of its most popular forms is cognitive-behavioral therapy, a major topic of this eBook. It focuses on the behaviors and thoughts of patients. Later, we'll know more about it.

Cognitive Therapy

This approach focuses on what people think, not on what they do, although not entirely dismissing the latter. Therapists are convinced that dysfunctional thinking is the main reason why certain people act the way they do, apart from the norms of the society. The therapy is used to change the thoughts of people, so they can change their feelings and actions.

Major contributors to this type of therapy include Aaron Beck, an American psychiatrist considered as the father of cognitive therapy, and Albert Ellis, an American psychologist and also one of the founders of cognitive-behavior therapy.

Of all the forms of therapies, it is the last two categories that have been proactive for the past recent years. It is to this effect that we discuss the third wave of psychotherapy. It is a group of emerging behavior and cognitive therapies that have shown significant improvements in the lives of people who have undergone such treatments. Very effective they are that they can be used to strengthen your brain, memory, and emotions. Very efficient they are that they can reshape your life and empower you to face life's challenges.

However, while the topic of third wave psychotherapies is long, we will attempt to discuss it in a brief chapter as follows. After which, we will look at each component: CBT, DBT, and ACT, teaching you how to use each in our lives.

CHAPTER 6.
THE THIRD WAVE PSYCHOTHERAPIES

To say that there have been many changes to psychotherapy since the early days of Sigmund Freud is an understatement. Like most approaches to mental health, it has evolved immensely, sprouting new branches and type. In the mental health profession, the changes and development of new approaches have been dubbed as *waves*.

Prior to the first wave was Freud's psychoanalysis and psychology. It was very traditional and old school, although at the time, it was groundbreaking. It was however, central to the therapist as an authority. Today, that relationship is no longer practiced, but the core ideas of psychoanalysis are much embedded in therapy sessions.

The First Wave

The first wave was set in motion in the 1950s by the increased demand for therapists. Going back a few chapters, you've learned that postwar America needed more mind doctors to treat returning traumatized soldiers and their affected families. Prevalent treatments available however, were not enough to combat the dysfunctional behaviors that damaged soldiers were manifesting.

According to Marina Williams, Substance Abuse Program Director at the Arbour Counseling Services in Boston and adjunct professor at the Grand Canyon University in Arizona, the first wave of psychotherapy criticized early therapies for the following reasons:

First, many therapists believed that sessions provided by traditional psychoanalysis were unstructured. They also noticed that patients' progress were very slow. Finally, although therapists who practiced psychoanalysis were in control of the therapy for each patient, they played a passive role to the overall cure and health of their wards.

The first wave was started by therapists who were against clinical conceptions that were widely used at the time. This was according to Steven Hayes, a leading clinical psychologist and major contributor to the third wave and author of the scientific journal article, Acceptance and Commitment Therapy, Relational Frame Theory, and the Third Wave of Behavioral and Cognitive Therapies (2004).

As mentioned in chapter 3, early therapists believed that only scientifically-proven and well-established treatments should be used and acknowledged by the psychiatric community. Any applied technologies that would come along should be rigorously tested with its basic principles specified thoroughly. In summary, early therapy was:

- Past and disease-oriented
- Focused on patient's pathology and deficits
- Examined past causes of trauma
- Therapist as the expert
- Theory-driven
- Therapies included psychoanalysis, psychodynamic, family of original therapy work and treatments, and genetic and biochemical therapies

However, contemporary therapists observed that not all clinical traditions were scientifically established. There was weak scientific evidence, vague specifications, and poorly-linked principles. These thoughts were shared among foremost and new behavior therapists, creating a unity within the field of behavior therapy and analysis.

The first wave however, prevailed until the 1960s.

The Second Wave

The second wave of psychotherapy appealed more to clients, although they didn't get to receive valuable insight in psychoanalysis as the early therapy did. The new set of therapies is more goal-directed and short term. More importantly to clients, the second wave of therapies enabled them to take control of their treatments. It includes modern therapies including behavioral and cognitive therapies.

Mental health professionals have argued which therapy is effective since the introduction of the new wave of therapies. Repeatedly though, various research have proven that all types of therapies are equally effective. It's generally up to the individual therapist which treatment to choose that will work best for patients. Clients however, are particular about the type of therapy that they want to have, as opposed to therapists' unbiased choice about the style of treatment they want to use.

Therapists meanwhile, know that there is a specific form of therapy that works for each patient. Patients are aware of this as well. Still, patients are disappointed whenever a certain type of therapy, which they selected in the first place, doesn't work for them. Therapists on the other hand, blame the failure of a treatment to the lack of chemistry and better working relationship between patient and doctor.

In theory though, patients would have a good experience with their therapists if they went to a therapist that specializes with their particular case. Often however, patients find it tedious to seek a therapist that offers the right, appropriate treatment for them. In other words, the problem isn't about the lack of chemistry. It is more basic, but deeper than that.

When the second wave arrived, therapists believed it was the answer to this problem. It was characterized by the same efforts that guided change in the psychiatric world. Cognitive principles and social learning were introduced in the 1960s, bringing new therapies including Beck's cognitive therapy and Ellis' Rational Emotive Behavior Therapy (REBT), a form of Cognitive Behavioral Therapy.

In summary, the second wave was:

- Present and problem-oriented
- Focuses on current causes or maintenance
- In part, therapist is still the expert
- Also theory-driven
- Therapies included behavioral, CBT/cognitive, family/systems, Gestalt, and EMDR/energy therapies

For three decades, the second wave was observed to produce the same results as the first wave did. Successful as they were, the problem still wasn't solved. This called for the third wave.

The Third Wave

The third wave, according to Hayes, was a deviation from and an extension of the traditional approaches of CBT. It started around the 1990s, ending the 3 decade reign of the second wave of therapies.

The cognitive behavioral therapy was a genuine shift from Freudian psychoanalysis when it was invented by Beck. Both are distinct and in a similar way, both give patients distinct experiences. The third wave was distinct from these forms in that it involves acceptance interventions and mindfulness.

Dialectical Behavior Therapy (DBT), Acceptance and Commitment Therapy (ACT), and other mindfulness-based cognitive therapies, are innovative behavioral treatments that uses elements of both its predecessors.

Perhaps the most unique attribute to the third wave of therapies is its collaborative nature; both client and therapist are experts in the treatment. The patient is very involved in clarifying the concern or problem at hand, and how it should be resolved. The patient's participation could mean success to the individual therapeutic process.

In general, third wave therapies exhibit the following characteristics:

- Present-oriented, but significantly considers the future
- Focuses on the solution and not the problem or its causes
- Focuses on patient's resources and competence
- Individualized, rather than theory-based
- Narrative and uses collaborative language systems
- Emphasizes neurological plasticity

According to Peter Wilhelm of the University of Fribourg in Switzerland, the third wave can be summed up in the following:

- Combines new concepts with traditional behavioral therapies. New concepts include spirituality, personal values, mindfulness, acceptance, and metacognition.
- Emphasizes and promotes the overall health and well-being. The aim is to help people in living and experiencing satisfying, fuller lives.
- Focuses less on reducing emotional and psychological symptoms. Reducing symptoms is a bonus or "side-benefit."
- Ignores key assumptions typically significant to CBT. The assumption that feelings, thoughts, or distressing symptoms, must be changed in frequency and content to improve holistic wellbeing is no longer considered helpful in a therapy or overall treatment.

Wilhelm is the author of The Third Wave of Cognitive Behavior Therapy: How Efficacious Are Newly Developed Interventions. He has extensively researched and lectured about the human psychology and the psychotherapy treatment in his home country of Switzerland.

Hayes on the other hand, characterizes the third wave as the following:

- Redevelops previous wave therapies and use them to address domains previously emphasized by other forms of therapies
- Focuses on the importance of issues for both patients and clinicians
- Supports creation of a wide range of flexible and effective aptitudes to define problems rather than eliminate existing ones

Cochrane Review, a collection of high-quality, independent research findings aimed to help healthcare decision-making identifies 7 approaches as the third therapies. This list includes seven main categories:

1. Acceptance and commitment therapy (ACT)
2. Dialectical Behavior therapy (DBT)
3. Mindfulness-based cognitive therapy (MBCT)
4. Compassionate mind training (CMT)
5. Metacognitive therapy (MCT)
6. Functional analytic psychotherapy (FAP)
7. Behavioral activation (BA)

In general, intervention for the third wave focuses on modifying thought function instead of manipulating thought content.

CHAPTER 7.
CBT, DBT, AND ACT

Before we proceed with the next section of this eBook, let's look at the brief description of each of the components of the third wave psychotherapies.

Cognitive Behavioral Therapy (CBT)

Cognitive Behavioral Therapy, or CBT, is a form of psychotherapy that focuses on the relevance of our thoughts to what we feel and do. It is based on the idea that our thoughts, not the circumstances we're in, affect our emotions and actions. In other words, CBT is a therapy based on the idea that there is an interconnection between thoughts, emotions, and behaviors.

For example, you woke up thinking that you'd rather not go to work today. You'd be less likely to get up and get going. If you're less likely to start the day right, then you're more likely to feel unaccomplished and unmotivated. If you feel that way, you'll be more inclined to think negative thoughts, and that will make you feel sad and wouldn't want to get out of bed. And the cycle goes on. Fortunately with CBT, you can stop this kind of cycle.

CBT encourages change through thoughts and behavior. If you'll change these two, then you can change how you feel about the situation and act appropriately. This is one of the key skills that CBT teaches. If there are thoughts that are challenging and overwhelming for you, you have the option to re-frame those.

Different techniques are taught to patients on how to re-frame thoughts. One of these techniques is to write down your thoughts. This record can be used as an evidence of your thoughts from which you can create a balanced perspective. Once that is achieved, the intensity of your negative thoughts, and their outcome, is evaluated by your therapist. In turn, you therapist will help you improve those thoughts.

CBT is a directive and structured therapy. It involves homework on your part and education from your therapist. This means that your therapist will assist you in the process of recording your thoughts. Therapists can also assist patients with creating behavioral homework assignments. This is to help you achieve your treatment goals.

Compared to other forms of therapy, CBT is considered briefer. Typically, treatments average on about 16 sessions. It is a general approach focused on therapist-client collaboration and client learning. It is also used as an umbrella term that covers more specific types of therapies including: Dialectic Behavior Therapy, Rational Living Therapy, Rational Emotive Behavior Therapy, and Rational Behavior Therapy to name a few.

CBT Applications

CBT is used to treat a wide range of issues and problems. It has been effective in treating various mental health conditions. Aside from depression or anxiety disorders, CBT can also be used to treat:

- alcohol abuse
- panic disorder
- obsessive-compulsive disorder
- post-traumatic stress disorder
- eating disorders – these include anorexia and bulimia
- phobias
- sleep problems these include insomnia

CBT can also treat long-term health conditions, such as chronic fatigue syndrome and irritable bowel syndrome. However, CBT can't cure these conditions. It can only help people suffering from it to cope better with the symptoms.

Dialectical Behavior Therapy (DBT)

Dialectical Behavior Therapy, or DBT, is a form of cognitive-behavioral therapy that focuses on solving behavioral problems by incorporating dialectical processes and acceptance-based strategies. It is best suited with the needs of patients suffering from intense emotional distress, preventing them from leading and experiencing a good quality of life.

DBT was developed by American psychology researcher and author Marsha Linehan. She created the therapy as a result of her own struggles with schizophrenia and suicidal thoughts at a young age. She was institutionalized for her mental illness until the age of 18.

Convinced that CBT has left a gap that needed to be filled, Linehan developed DBT at the University of Washington years later. DBT consists of four key skill areas and main components: interpersonal skills training, distress tolerance, emotional regulation, and mindfulness training.

DBT treatment can be delivered in many ways, typically consisting of individual therapy sessions and/or DBT skills groups. For example, while some patients may complete individual therapy sessions without attending any skills group, others might opt group sessions without the individual therapy.

An individual therapy session consists of a one-on-one session with DBT therapist. This ensures that the patient's therapeutic needs are attended to. Over the course of the treatment, the therapist will also help the patient apply DBT skills on a daily basis, appropriately address daily struggles that should occur, and stay motivated.

DBT skills group on the other hand, encourage members to learn and practice skills with each other while they are led by a DBT therapist. Members provide mutual support for each other and listen as others share their experiences.

Therapists in a group session teach skills and lead members into group exercises. Each member is assigned with a homework which often involves practicing mindfulness exercises.

Group sessions are typically completed within six months. Weekly sessions are conducted with each one lasting up to more or less two hours. The length of each session depends on the needs of each member.

DBT Applications

DBT is applies to treat a wide range of issues and problems most prominently, borderline personality disorder. It is also well suited for addictions and eating disorders.

While DBT was initially developed as a treatment for borderline personality disorder, it has also been effective in treating patients with:

- Depression
- Post-traumatic stress disorder (PTSD)
- Bipolar disorder
- Substance abuse
- Bulimia
- Binge-eating

DBT skills can teach you to improve your ability to:

- communicate and interact with others
- be mindful of the present at any given moment

- tolerate negative emotions
- endure distress
- regulate your emotions

Acceptance And Commitment Therapy (ACT)

Acceptance and Commitment Therapy, or ACT, is a form of therapy that draws from mindfulness practice and cognitive behavioral psychotherapy. It is also known as a *contextual psychotherapy* because it encourages patients to exhibit values-based positive behaviors even if they are experiencing negative sensations, emotions, or thoughts. In other words, it helps patients increase their psychological flexibility.

As a third wave Cognitive Behavioral Therapy (CBT), ACT (said as one word) is strongly connected to the power of behavioral change. However, ACT differs from CBT. It can change the relationship you have with your thoughts rather than change them directly. ACT promotes the notion that you don't have to do anything with your thoughts to push change in your behavior.

ACT focuses on mindfulness, diffusion of challenging thoughts, and acceptance of unpleasant emotions. With ACT, your efforts are concentrated to moving you towards a momentous life by helping your learn to separate yourself from your thoughts. Your efforts are based on your committed action towards establishing your values.

ACT mindfulness skills have 3 categories:

1. *Acceptance*: enables patients to make room for sensations, urges, and painful feelings, and allowing them to easily come and go
2. *Defusion*: enables patients to let go of and distance from unhelpful thoughts, memories, and beliefs
3. *Contact with the present moment*: enables patients to fully engage, with an attitude of curiosity and openness, with their here-and-now experience

ACT can be delivered in many different ways:

- Ultra-brief ACT – ACT can be highly effective even in one or two twenty to thirty-minute sessions. A good example is treatment by Kirk Strosahl, co-founder of ACT, in primary care medical settings.
- Brief ACT – ACT is done with only four sessions at 1-hour each. A good example is treatment by Patty Bach, assistant professor of psychology at the Illinois Institute of Technology, used on patients with schizophrenia.
- Medium-term ACT – ACT is completed for a total of eight hours. An example is a protocol for chronic pain by professor of psychology at Uppsala University in Sweden, JoAnne Dahl.
- Long-term ACT – ACT takes forty sessions at 2-hour each. This is very effective in treating patients with borderline personality disorder (BPD). One of the only few known users of long-term ACT is Spectrum, the Personality Disorder (clinic) Service in the state of Victoria in Australia.

Note: Therapy Affects The Brain
According to a study published in the American Journal of Psychology in 1998, several decades of research has revealed that all mental processes derive from brain mechanism.

This means that any change in our psychological processes is reflected by changes in the functions or structures of the brain.

It doesn't come as a surprise then that the outcome and effects of these therapies that brings about change in an individual have been studied on the social and psychological levels. Changes in social functioning, personality, psychological abilities, and symptoms were carefully measured. These changes are in a way, brain mechanisms.

Chapter 8.
Cognitive Behavioral Therapy (CBT)

The primary objective of CBT is to modify our thought patterns, our attitudes, our beliefs, and our behavior to help us overcome our hardships and work towards our goals.

Beck, the founder of CBT, practiced psychoanalysis for years until he noticed that many of his clients have internal dialogues that supported his theory about the strong connection between feelings and thoughts. So, he changed his way of therapy to help his patients identify, understand, then manage their emotions.

Beck discovered that a mixture of behavioral strategies and cognitive therapy provided the best results for his patients. In working out with the emerging therapy, the founder of CBT established the foundations of today's most important form of psychotherapy.

This method of psychotherapy is not intended for long-term involvement but concentrates more on assisting patients to achieve their immediate goals. Many CBT sessions can only last from five to 10 months that involve at least 50 minutes for every weekly session.

CBT is a type of treatment that requires a hands-on approach. It requires both the therapist and the client to invest their time and focus on the process. The treatment rarely works without both parties participating actively in the sessions. Together, they form a team to determine the problems that the client has to resolve and identify possible strategies to tackle the issues.

CBT as an Effective Treatment for Cognitive Distortions

Most CBT treatments today are used to resolve issues on cognitive distortions, which refer to the thoughts that support the negative emotions or thought patterns. These are known as flawed methods of thinking, which allows our mind to form assumed realities that are not true. Cognitive distortions are also known as thinking errors.

Psychologists identified 15 primary forms of cognitive distortions that could affect even those who consider their thinking as balanced.

1. Fallacy of Heaven's Reward

This form of cognitive distortion is characterized by the thought of expecting that any self-denial or sacrifice will be rewarded. This can be described as the belief in karma, and we expect that karma will always instantly pay off when we do good things. The distortion can be negative if we feel bitterness because we failed to receive the expected reward.

2. Overgeneralization

This refers to the selection of a single point in time or incident and using it as the only piece of evidence for a wider conclusion. For example, an amateur salesperson could be struggling on his job because of rejections, but instead of moving on to the next prospect and trying again, he concluded that he is terrible at the job and will never sell a single product again.

3. Mislabeling / Global Labeling

Mislabeling, also known as global labeling, is a form of extreme generalization wherein a person may generalize a single or several qualities or instances into a worldwide perception. For instance, if we don't complete a particular task, we may think that we are a complete failure not only in a certain area but in general. Meanwhile, if a person we just met says something that is not within our belief system, we could conclude that the person is up to no good in general.

This form of cognitive distortion is specific to using emotional and exaggerated language, such as concluding that a mother is irresponsible when she opted to leave her children in the care of a nanny so she could go to a party.

4. Fallacies of Control
This type of cognitive distortion refers to the thoughts of people who think that everything that happens to them could be the outcome of external forces or because of their own actions. There are instances that what happens to us is caused by the forces that we don't have any control, and sometimes because of our actions. The fallacy here is in the assumption that it is always either of the two. People could assume that the work quality is because of working with people we don't agree with, or on the other hand, that each error that someone else is making is caused by something that we are doing.

5. Shoulds
This refers to the explicit or implicit rules that we have established upon us or the people around us on how they should behave. If other people violate our established rules, we may feel bad. We also feel the same if we break our own rules.

For instance, if you are on a diet and you have established the rule of saying no to dessert, then during lunch you give in to your desire of savoring chocolate fudge, you would probably feel guilty and feel bad that you have broken your rule. On the other hand, if you have always had this mindset that the customer is always right, and you encounter a sales representative that tries to argue with you, you may get angry.

6. Filtering
Filtering is one of the most common forms of cognitive distortion. This refers to the way most of us may ignore all the good and positive things that happened in our day so we only concentrate on the negative side.

People who have established filters in their minds tend to focus on the negative aspects of their lives despite being surrounded by good things.

7. Jumping to Conclusions

Like overgeneralization, this form of cognitive distortion refers to the flawed logic in how people make wrong conclusions. But rather than overgeneralizing a single incident, jumping to conclusion refers to the person's tendency to be certain even with the absence of solid evidence. We might think that our coworker does not like us with only the smallest of hint, or we may be persuaded that our fears could be right before even we have the opportunity to explore our options.

8. Black and White or Polarized Thinking

Polarized thinking is all about the perception of seeing only black and white. This means that the person doesn't see any grey area. This can be described as an all-or-nothing thinking with no space for nuance or sophistication. If a person fails to perform with perfection in several areas, then he may see himself as a complete failure rather than simply not skilled in a single area.

9. Personalization

This form of cognitive distortion refers to the belief of some people that everything they are doing could affect other people or external events, regardless of how illogical it may seem. People who are suffering from this form of distortion may feel that they have an unreasonably crucial role in the negative things that are happening around them.

For example, you were working with a team to develop advertisement content. Your boss pitched it to a client and the client was dissatisfied. You end up blaming yourself, believing that if you hadn't suggested the particular typeface that ended up on the final product, the outcome would have been different.

10. Always Being Right

Even though many of us enjoy being right, this cognitive distortion makes people think that being wrong is not acceptable, and we should always be right all the time. Some people may believe that being right is more important than being objective or fair, the humility to admit mistake when we have made them, or the feelings of people around us.

11. Blame Game

There are numerous ways that we could assign responsibility or explain the results when things don't happen according to on our expectations. The most common way to do this is through the blame game, in which we may blame other people for acting a specific way or for making us feel bad. This is considered as a form of cognitive distortion because it is not reasonable to blame other people for anything that we act or feel.

12. Fallacy of Change

This form of cognitive distortion is grounded in expecting the people around us to change according to our preferences and needs. This lies in the same alley that our happiness depends on other people and their inability or unwillingness to change, even if we keep our demands, make us unhappy. This is unhealthy because we should assume the responsibility for our own happiness.

13. Minimizing or Magnifying Catastrophe

Minimizing or magnifying catastrophe is a form of cognitive distortion involving expectations that the worst may happen or has already happened depending on a minimal incident that could be totally unrelated to negative circumstances.

For example, you might have committed a minor mistake at work, and you are already convinced that it will derail the whole operations, and your supervisor will be angry and will recommend to your boss to fire you. On the other hand, it could also take the form of minimizing important accomplishments in life such as a big promotion or a big goal finally achieved at work.

14. Fallacy of Fairness
Human beings have the natural tendency to be concerned about being fair. However, this concern could be taken to extremes. It is important to be aware of the reality that life is not always fair. People who go through life looking for fairness may end up being unhappy and resentful. There will always be instances that things will not happen according to our desires, regardless of how fair it would seem.

15. Emotional Reasoning
This cognitive distortion is characterized by the belief that if we feel a specific way, it should be true. For instance, if we feel that we are not good at our job, we must be really not fit for the task. It is evident that our emotions do not always indicate the truth based on objective assumption. However, it could be difficult to ignore our feelings.

People who are suffering from low self-esteem and anxiety are vulnerable to being entrapped in an endless limbo of negative thoughts. Through CBT, you can be aware when you are being dragged down by negative thinking, which could result in a self-fulfilling predicament.

For instance, an office staff member who thinks that his boss hates him may begin to have physical manifestations like sweating at the mere idea of being near his boss. So, he avoids meeting his boss that makes him even more left out in the office and eventually could result in more negative thinking that he is really hopeless in the workplace. The damaging cycle will then leave the person feeling anxious or depressed. When the initial thought was managed properly, the whole cycle of negativity that follows could have been prevented.

CBT can help you become more aware when you start being swayed by thinking errors. This form of psychotherapy can also teach you how to analyze your thoughts so they will not trigger a vicious cycle of negative stream, and it will also help you in replacing your thoughts with thinking that are more balanced and reasonable.

These cognitive distortions could be strong habits that you are engaging deep within your subconscious, and a CBT expect could help you resolve specific issues and provide you with the tools you need to modify your way of thinking to help you resolve any mental or emotional issues you have.

For example, if you have noticed that you are prone to polarized thinking, you should try to look for the in-between. Remind yourself that there is typically a wider range of results between a complete disaster and absolute perfection. Rare is the chance that you will encounter an all or nothing scenario.

If you have the tendency to think of something as always or never, could you identify the exceptions? Otherwise, it is not really always or never. Ask yourself if it is really bad or you are just being extreme. Also, try to look for other ways to look at a particular situation.

Once you become aware that you have these thinking errors, you should avoid feeling bad. Accepting the fact that you are experiencing a cognitive distortion is the initial step that you have to take so you can resolve your issues. The workbook can be helpful when you are experiencing negative thoughts, but a psychotherapist who is experienced in CBT could help you challenge and improve your thinking patterns using a more personalized treatment.

Important CBT Tools and Techniques

There are various techniques and tools used in CBT, and you'd be surprised to know that many of them are already a part of our daily lives. The tools and techniques described in these sections are among the most common and effective practices in CBT, primarily in overcoming different cognitive distortions.

Cognitive Restructuring

When you start becoming more aware of the thinking errors or the unreasonable perceptions that you often have, you can learn more about how negative thinking is affecting you and why it is affecting your belief system. Once you discover a belief that is damaging your wellbeing, you can start challenging it.

For instance, if you think that you should have a high-paying job so people around you will recognize and respect you, and you end up losing a high-paying job, your self-perception could be destroyed.

Rather than succumbing to this flawed notion that could lead you to think illogical negative thoughts about yourself, you can take your chance to think about the traits that make a person respectable, which is an assumption that might not have explicitly crossed your mind before.

Unraveling Errors In Your Thinking

This technique is actually a primary objective of CBT, and you can even do this even without the help of a professional psychotherapist. To unravel the errors in your thinking, you should first be familiar of specific errors you are most prone to committing. A part of this may involve identifying and challenging our damaging default thinking that usually falls into one of the categories that we have described earlier.

Keeping a Journal

This strategy is a process to gather more information about our thoughts and moods. Keeping a journal may include the specific time that we began feeling a particular mood, its source, its intensity, and how we have reacted to it, among other factors. This process could help us in identifying our thinking and mood patterns, recognize them, and figure out how we can manage them effectively.

Progressive Muscle Relaxation (PMR)

Those who are practicing mindfulness are familiar with this technique. Like the body scan, this strategy will enable you to relax specific groups of muscles one at a time, until your entire body is already relaxed. You can use audio recordings, a short mindfulness clip online, but even your own mind will do. PMR is quite helpful in calming your nerves. Practicing PMR will allow you to clear your mind so you can easily identify your cognitive distortions and resolve your issues.

Interceptive Exposure

This CBT technique is designed for immediate treatment of anxiety or panic attacks. This involves the exposure of the patient to fearful physical sensations to extract responses, activate any damaging beliefs connected with the sensations, allow new realizations on these sensations, and sustain the sensation without avoidance or distraction. This is ideal for patients who are suffering the symptoms of anxiety and see that panic attacks are not harmful, even though they are generally not a pleasant experience.

Script Playing

This CBT technique is particularly beneficial for people who are suffering from anxiety and fear. In this strategy, you will be exposed to anxiety or crippling fear, and you will be asked to perform a type of thought experiment wherein you need to visualize the result of the worst case scenario. Allowing this scenario to be played out in mind could help you accept the fact that while there is a possibility that your fears will happen, it is more likely that everything will be fine.

Relaxed Breathing

Relaxed breathing is a technique that is not completely unique to CBT. Those who are practicing mindfulness are quite familiar with it. There are different ways to calm your mind and body. This includes scripts, videos, audio records, and guided/unguided imagery. Encouraging calm and regularity to your breath will enable you to resolve your problems to find balance, and allow more rational and effective decision making.

This technique could help people who are suffering from different mental health concerns such as panic disorder, OCD, depression, and anxiety. They can also be performed even without the assistance of a professional psychotherapist.

Exposure and Response Prevention
Exposure and response prevention is a CBT technique that can help people who are suffering from Obsessive-Compulsive Disorder (OCD). Performing this strategy requires exposing the patient to whatever it is that usually triggers their compulsive behavior. This technique can be combined with journaling as the patient is encouraged to write about the experience.

Nightmare Exposure and Rescripting
This CBT technique is ideal for patients who are suffering from constant nightmares. It is usually compared to interceptive exposure because the bad dreams that the patient usually experience can stir relevant emotions. When the emotion has been triggered, the psychotherapist can help the patient to figure out the preferred emotions then work together to create a new image that can be used to elicit the preferred emotion.

Chapter 9.
CBT and Cognitive Dissonance

Cognitive dissonance, also known as cognitive disharmony, refers to the state of conflict within our mind, in which we are faced with two conflicting beliefs at the same time. The human brain is designed to eliminate disharmony as much as possible, and it fulfills this role by changing the way we perceive or feel about certain things.

Understanding cognitive dissonance is vital for the effective use of CBT because this can be used as a powerful motivational tool to change a person's behavior.

All of us have already experienced a form of cognitive dissonance at some point. In general, if you believe that you are a good person, and you do something bad, the discomfort that you feel is caused by the dissonance. The common signs of cognitive dissonance include:

- Discomfort
- Guilt
- Shame
- Avoidance
- Rationalization
- Ignoring the facts

The disharmony within our minds is usually most intense if we are highly committed to a certain belief, but our behavior follows the opposite direction. For example, if 30-year-old Lucia believes she is an independent woman, but still lives with her parents, she will experience a great deal of tension. In response, the brain will try to justify or deny, or change her attitude and beliefs – all to reduce the tension:

- *My parents will not allow me to leave home. They need me.*
- *How can I survive if I live alone?*
- *I am comfortable living with my parents anyway.*
- *I love my parents and I want to spend more time with them.*
- *I help in paying the bills.*

Even though Lucia might have not initially agreed with these reasons, her mind justifies her situation to weaken the disharmony she feels. Cognitive dissonance is such a powerful tool because no one really likes to feel disharmony.

Forms of Cognitive Dissonance

Cognitive dissonance can happen to anyone in almost all facets of life. It happens in relationships, in the workplace, in the supermarket, and even during your break time.

Cognitive Dissonance in Relationships

One common example of how cognitive dissonance influences relationships is when people are dating. For example, Lawrence really likes a woman who values money. When he first met her girlfriend Stacy, she seemed practical and seemed to know how to save – but it turns out that she's spendthrift who often requests for gifts that are expensive.

There were red flags like the fact that she always seemed to be chasing after some designer bag. "Maybe that designer bag is just a one-time thing." That was the first thing he said when he noticed. She's also always worried about maxing out her credit cards, but Lawrence ignored them. She also tends to choose expensive restaurants but does not offer to split the bill. He told himself that perhaps, Stacy just likes luxury -- nothing wrong with a woman who has appreciation for the finer things in life.

Ignoring the obvious facts is an indicator of dissonance. Rather than admitting that Stacy may not be a good fit as a partner for him, Lawrence convinced himself that she will eventually change.

Cognitive dissonance is quite common in relationships that are abusive. Consider the couple, Robert and Diane, who have been dating for six years, but only married for a year. The marriage is happy and filled with passion. But one day, Robert slapped Diane during an argument.

Diane -- who thought she really knew her husband – started to experience dissonance. She abhors violence against women and has sworn that she will never let herself be victimized. But she found herself trying to rationalize his behavior. "He was too drunk, and I might have pushed my limits," she said. "He is kind and cares a lot about me when he is not drunk."

It is common for people to rationalize bad behavior and choose to stay in the relationship despite the abuses.

There are cases in which people are oppressed in a narcissistic relationship, but they end up forming a codependent relationship with the abuser. Cognitive dissonance causes a phenomenon known as trauma bonding. For instance, if someone is experiencing Stockholm Syndrome, they usually justify the abuse despite the fact that they are just rationalizing to cope with the situation.

The victim of the narcissistic abuse will start to believe that staying with the oppressor is important for survival. If they think the relationship is threatened, the victim may panic and become anxious. This is why some people resist undergoing any form of psychotherapy session as they are often afraid to hear the truth.

Cognitive Dissonance in the Workplace

Many of us have already experienced cognitive dissonance in the workplace. Consider the following examples:

At the office, Mary (who sees herself as an honest person) is not monitored regularly. Each time she takes her one-hour lunch break, she actually extends for another 30 minutes. Instead of believing she's stealing money because she is getting paid for the time she is not working, she reasons that she is overworking anyway and uses the extra time to unwind before heading back to work again.

Fred is the HR manager for a large company. One day, he was ordered to fire an employee for misconduct without enough evidence to support the claim. Because Fred strongly believes in fairness and justice, the unsupported claim from his superior will result in dissonance. The dilemma will cause tension because he may even lose his job if he fails to execute the order, even though it is clearly unethical to do so.

Cognitive Dissonance and Consumer Decisions

As adults, we want to believe that we are capable of making good decisions. But a simple shopping experience can create a dissonance if something that we purchased which we thought was good turns out to be bad.

For example, Gary would like to believe he's an environmentalist. He likes to help in eco-friendly causes and even volunteers for a local group supporting environmental initiatives. He bought a new car, and it turns out that it was a gas guzzler. Upon learning this, he struggled with the idea that he will drive a car that is harmful to the environment. He decided to sell the car and instead use public transport.

Meanwhile, Wilma declared that saving more money is one of her New Year's resolutions, but she ended up buying a designer coat using her credit card. Admittedly, she spent way more money than she can afford and so, she feels buyer's remorse. Instead of being bothered by the undesirable emotion caused by the dissonance in her mind, she decides that the bag will last longer than her cheap ones. Besides, the bag is really a nice bit of eye candy – maybe it will help her project a better image of herself at work (and during dates).

In a 2003 study published in the Journal of Product & Brand Management, it was revealed that consumers usually use three coping mechanisms to reduce their cognitive dissonance when they think they are overspending:

1. Look for more information – they try to find more information that will justify their purchase
2. Change their attitude – for example, they may try to re-evaluate the worth of the purchase
3. Downplay the significance of what they spent – "I can earn the money again!"

Cognitive Dissonance and Addiction

With the sheer amount of information available today, people surely know that smoking and drinking too much alcohol can heavily damage their health. But still, people are into different forms of substance abuse. They are already informed and many of them understand the risks, but their actions create cognitive dissonance.

Laura is a doctor. She understands how damaging smoking is. Now that she is already 35 years old, she smokes at least three cigarettes a day to cope with stress, and even takes cocaine occasionally especially when she is depressed. *"My grandmother used to smoke a pack a day, and she lived to be 98!"*

By justifying her behavior, Laura was able to reduce the cognitive dissonance. Laura is trying to change her frame of mind so she will not feel bad about the discomfort caused by the dissonance.

Cognitive Dissonance and Spirituality

Religion and spirituality also play a vital role in the formation of the Cognitive Dissonance Theory. After all, religion influenced many of the values we hold dear today – love, honesty, charity, generosity, sacrifice, and service, among others.

For people who are strongly grounded in their life principles based on the tenets of their religion, intense dissonance could happen especially if they are faced with a situation and their behavior was against their belief.

For example, Joe is a pastor at a local Christian church. He believes in the sanctity of life, which is much in line with his pastoral career. When he watched the evening news, he learned about a group of drug dealers killed during a police operation.

He thought they deserved to be killed, but he felt a strong dissonance within himself. He justifies his thoughts by telling himself that the drug dealers have destroyed the lives of hundreds of people, and that they deserved to be punished.

Cognitive dissonance can also happen if we have seen certain things damaged our belief system. For example, Jesse really looked up to the humility and spirituality embodied by Buddhist monks. But on a trip to Thailand, he saw a group of monks drinking alcohol and was even rude when they were drunk. He experienced cognitive dissonance as he strongly believed that Buddhist monks should not behave that way.

The Role of Cognitive Dissonance in CBT

As already mentioned at the beginning of this Chapter, understanding cognitive dissonance is vital for the effective use of CBT. Psychotherapists specializing in CBT can use cognitive dissonance as a powerful motivational tool to influence the behavior of a person, especially those who are trying to cope with the effects of abusive relationships.

Cognitive dissonance is particularly helpful in cognitive restructuring. When we become more aware of the presence of disharmony in our mind, we can learn more about how the dissonance can affect our decisions. When we are aware that we have the tendency to reduce the dissonance, we may choose to challenge it and choose a more beneficial action. For example, if you are in the shoes of Pastor Joe and your thoughts (drug dealers deserve to die) are not aligned with your belief (life is sacred), being aware that your mind will try to justify the dissonance will allow you to strengthen your grounding on your principles.

Some CBT specialists also use cognitive dissonance as a vital tool in script playing. People who are suffering from anxiety disorder are often prescribed to work on their cognitive dissonance and visualize in their mind the consequences of their actions if they are not in line with their beliefs. Allowing specific scenarios to play out in the mind can help people to realize the possible outcome of their decisions if they continue with their behavior.

Reducing Cognitive Dissonance

The idea of cognitive dissonance was first explored by the psychologist Leon Festinger who focused on how we try to reach internal consistency. He also suggested that people usually have their internal need to make sure that their actions and beliefs are consistent.

Festinger also defined three ways to reduce the disharmony in our minds:

1. Changing the value or importance of the contradicting belief
2. Identify a new belief that will support the action
3. Changing the action altogether

Let's use the example of Lawrence, the pastor, to further explore these three ways:
Belief: I am looking for a woman who knows the value of money
Action: Dating a woman who is a spendthrift.

So what can Lawrence do? He could use any of the three ways to reduce the dissonance as pointed out above.

- Change the value or importance of the contradicting belief as in:
  "It doesn't matter if she's materialistic, to be honest"
  "She might love luxurious things, but she's really fun and pretty"

- Identify a new belief that will support the action
  "If she spends more time with me, she might learn the values that are really important for me"
  "Proper handling of money can be learned. If I devote more time to sharing my principles with her, maybe she will change."

- Changing the action altogether.
  "I am done with her"
  "I don't want to be with a woman who lives way beyond her means."

Let's use another example – this time the case of Pastor Joe.
Belief: Life is sacred.
Action: Rallying for the death of the drug dealers.

- Change the value or importance of the contradicting belief
  "They deserve death. Destroying the lives of innocent people through drug addiction is a grave sin."

- Identify a new belief that will support the action
  "*My brothers at the Church abhor drug dealers.*"
  "*Drug addicts deserve help, but drug dealers are the worst scums of the Earth.*"

- Changing the action altogether.
  "*I should be ashamed of my thoughts. Life is sacred, regardless of the sin.*"

Exercises:

1. Think of a recent cognitive dissonance that you have experienced. How did you manage the disharmony? What were your specific actions to reduce the dissonance?

2. Practice coming up with ways to reduce dissonance using the other examples above as your guide.

Chapter 10.
Overcoming Negative Thinking and Anxiety with CBT

Getting rid of negative thinking and anxiety is easier said than done. As a matter of fact, studies reveal that even if you tell people to avoid thinking too much about a specific topic, it makes it even more difficult to get the thought pattern out of their minds.

However, indulging in negative thinking and re-running thoughts over and over in your head could be counterproductive and uncomfortable. In some instances, it could even result in chronic depression.

CBT can help you get away from staying too much on negative thinking by refocusing your mind on something positive. Through a series of therapy sessions, anyone who is heavily affected by negative thinking can benefit from rewiring the brain.

Most people who experience anxiety or depression caused by negative thinking should try CBT so the issues can be addressed immediately. Studies suggest that people who are depressed don't usually respond well to self-help techniques. Hence, it is recommended to attend CBT sessions for at least six weeks. A CBT specialist can teach you certain techniques that could help in counteracting the negative thought patterns associated with depression.

Common CBT Strategies to Help You Manage Negative Thinking

Identify the Root Problem that Causes Negative Thinking

It is important to find the problem and brainstorm for possible solutions. Talking with a psychotherapist and keeping a journal could help in discovering the root of negative thinking.

Write down every idea you have in mind. Think about the things that are bothering you and find ways to address the problem. Hopelessness is a trademark of depression. This is the belief that nothing can be better. Making a list of things that you can do to improve your current situation could help you to reduce the uncomfortable feeling.

For instance, if you are combating depression, there are many things you can do such as adopting a pet, signing up for a local club based on your interest, volunteering to a charity you care for and a lot more to avoid sinking further and deeper into it.

Keep a Journal to Help You Fight Negative Thinking

After determining triggers and aggravating factors for your depression, the next step is to be vigilant about the bad thoughts that often pop into your head to overpower the positive ones.

In your journal, try writing a self-statement to fight every negative thought. Take note of your self-statements and read them to yourself whenever you are being pulled down by your negative thoughts. As you go along with this discipline, you will eventually develop new associations that will replace negative thinking with positive ones.

But you should remember that self-statement must not be too far from negative thoughts as the mind might not be able to accept it. For instance, when the negative thought is "I'm so sad today" you should not try to fight it with. "I am really happy today." That would just be a complete lie. A better self-statement will be, *"It's okay to be sad. This is just an emotion. This too shall pass. And tomorrow will be a better day."*

This statement implies that it is fine to bump up the level of joy you may feel and your mind will be in check to safeguard you from disappointment. It is healthy to recognize the part of our body and mind that are trying to help us cope with negative emotions.

Learn to Accept Disappointments

It is crucial to accept disappointment as part of our lives. The way we respond could affect how easily we can move forward. A teenager who is going through a bad breakup may blame trivial things such as simple acne, thinking, "There is no point in trying to look good. No one will like me."

A better approach is to allow yourself to experience disappointment and be reminded that there are things that are beyond our control. Focus instead on the things that you can control.

Take note of the details of your current situation, the lessons you have learned from the experience, and what you could do differently next time. This could help you move forward and be more positive about your future.

Look for Fresh Opportunities for Positive Thinking

Even those who enter a room and instantly think that they hate the furniture can probably rewire their brain to find at least three things in the room that they like. One easy technique is to set a phone reminder at least three times a day to rewire your thoughts for positive thinking. If you have a family or friend who also needs to manage their negative thinking, you can choose to buddy up and watch each other. This way, your team can share your thoughts and experiences.

Evening Reflection

You can also combat negative thinking by reflecting the best parts that happened every day. Ideally, you can write down in your journal the things that you are thankful for. Keeping tab of your positive thoughts, and also sharing these thoughts with your loved ones could help you to develop new associations in your mind to build new pathways. With this technique, you can wake up in the morning feeling refreshed and ready to overcome any challenge of the day.

How CBT Can Help You Manage Anxiety Disorder

If your life is heavily affected by incapacitating phobia, unrelenting worries, obsessive thoughts, or panic attacks, you might be suffering from anxiety disorder. Through CBT, you can manage anxiety problems by harnessing your mind to conquer your fears and take control of your anxiety. Before we further discuss CBT and how it can help you get relief from too much worrying, let us first understand anxiety disorder.

What is Anxiety Disorder?

Anxiety disorder is one of the most common mental disorders and is characterized by fear, worry, and feelings of uneasiness. Even though humans have the natural tendency to feel anxious, an individual with an anxiety disorder could experience uncomfortable levels of anxiety that is usually beyond reason.

For instance, an average man may feel worried before going into a job interview, but a person who has anxiety disorder may feel worried every time he goes to work. This condition is believed to be underdiagnosed. More often than not, those who are suffering from anxiety disorder are not aware that they have a treatable illness.

Individuals who are experiencing anxiety disorder also suffer from related mental health conditions like depression. If left untreated, the condition could lead to self-harm and even suicide.

The symptoms of anxiety disorder vary according to the type of illness, but the condition is generally characterized by the inability to sleep well, irritability, inability to focus, a sense of impending danger or doom and physical symptoms such as heart palpitations, sweating, or muscle tension. Those with anxiety disorder also tend to experience feelings of helplessness and restlessness.

Anxiety disorder is also characterized by the person's inability to perform his daily activities. Those who suffer from the condition often have reduced quality of life.

Specific forms of anxiety disorder are included in the updated Diagnostic and Statistical Manual of Mental Disorders. (DSMMD). This includes obsessive-compulsive disorder (OCD), generalized anxiety disorder, panic disorder, post-traumatic stress disorder, agoraphobia, social anxiety disorder, and even simple phobia.

Social anxiety disorder is the most common type of anxiety disorder and the symptoms usually show before age 20. Common phobias - such as fear of cockroaches - are also quite typical with more than 1 in 10 people suffering from a specific phobia.

For treatment of anxiety disorder, studies reveal that therapy is often one of the most effective techniques. This is because therapy - not similar to most medications - can treat beyond the symptoms of the disorder. CBT can help you discover the deeper causes of your fears and worries, gain new perspective on things, learn how to be calm amidst panic attacks, and build better problem-solving and coping skills. CBT can provide you the tools to help you manage your anxiety disorder.

There are different forms of anxiety disorder, and CBT can be customized based on specific concerns and symptoms. If you are experiencing panic attacks, for example, your CBT treatment will be quite different compared to someone who has obsessive-compulsive disorder.

In addition, the length of the treatment will also rely on the form and intensity of your anxiety disorder. However, most CBT techniques for anxiety disorder are quite short-term. In fact, the American Psychological Association prescribes only 8 to 10 CBT sessions for people who have anxiety disorders.

Cognitive Behavioral Therapy

Many various forms of treatments are used for anxiety disorder relief. However, the leading techniques are CBT and other related treatments such as exposure therapy. Each treatment can be used as a standalone therapy or as part of a regimen.

CBT is a common form of treatment often prescribed for people who are suffering from anxiety disorders. Research reveals that CBT is an effective approach in the treatment of generalized anxiety disorder, social anxiety disorder, phobias, and panic disorder among other mental health conditions. CBT can address distortions and negative patterns in the way we perceive the world and our own image.

Remember, the fundamental concept of CBT is that our own mindset - not our environment – can affect our emotions. To put this simply, it is not our current circumstance that will set how we feel, but how we perceive the situation. For instance, let's say that you have been selected to present a sales pitch to an important client. Work on at least three different approaches in thinking about the opportunity and how your thoughts could affect the way you feel.

Scenario: You Need to Present a Major Sales Pitch
Thought No. 1: *The opportunity is exciting. I love talking to a client who is really in need of our service.*
Emotions: Excited, Happy

Thought No. 2: *Presentations are not my alley. I'd rather stay in the office and prepare the report for someone else who is better than me at speaking in front of people.*
Emotions: Neutral

Thought No. 3: *I don't know what to say. What if I mess up the presentation? My boss will hate me.*
Emotions: Apprehensive

As you would notice, different individuals could feel different emotions from the same situation. This can all depend on each person's beliefs, attitudes, and expectations. For those who are suffering from anxiety disorders, negative thinking could also fuel negative emotions of fear and anxiety. CBT's goal is for anxiety to determine and rectify these negative beliefs and thoughts. The main idea is that if you alter how you think, you can also reshape your emotions.

The 3-Step CBT Technique of Challenging Your Thoughts

Cognitive restructuring - also known as thought challenging - is a CBT process wherein you need to challenge your negative thoughts that will only feed your anxiety, and instead replacing them with more realistic and positive thoughts. This process involves three specific steps:

Step 1 - Identify Your Negative Thoughts

People who suffer from anxiety disorder perceive situations as more harmful as they really are. For example, for someone with fear of germs, shaking hands is perceived as a high-risk activity. Even though this is often seen as an irrational fear, understanding these thinking patterns could be a challenge. One way to work around is to continue asking yourself what you were thinking when you began feeling anxious. Your CBT specialist can assist you in completing this step.

Step 2 - Challenge Negative Thinking

Next, your CBT specialist will assist you to effectively assess your thoughts that are causing your anxiety problem. This may include scrutinizing the validity of your worrisome thoughts, evaluating beliefs that are not helpful, and checking out the reality of negative predictions. The most common approaches for challenging negative thinking involve thinking about the real changes that what you are worried about may not really happen, comparing the advantages and disadvantages of anxiety, performing experiments, or avoiding the root cause of your fear.

Step 3 - Replace Negative Thinking with Realistic Thinking
After successfully identifying the negative distortions and irrational predictions in your negative thoughts, the next step is to replace them with fresh thoughts that are more positive and realistic. Your CBT specialist can also assist you in coming up with more accurate and relaxing statements that you can repeat to yourself when you are about to experience a situation that will usually cause you anxiety.

To better understand the mechanism of challenging your negative thoughts in CBT, let's examine this short example:

Betty doesn't want to keep jogging because she's worried about how she looks when she runs, and she thinks that everyone would laugh at her. Her CBT specialist asked her to make a list of her negative thoughts, figure out cognitive distortions, and work around with a more logical statement. Take a look at the results:

Negative Thought No. 1: What if I look silly when I go jogging?
Negative Distortion: Thinking about the worst case scenario
More Realistic Thought: No one ever told me I look silly.

Negative Thought No. 2: If I look silly, it will be terrible!
Negative Distortion: Blowing things out of proportion
More Realistic Thought: I am doing this for my health. That is not terrible.

Negative Thought No. 3: People might laugh at me
Negative Distortion: Jumping to conclusions
More Realistic Thought: Other people's opinion is none of my business

Certainly, it can be challenging to replace negative thoughts with more realistic ways of thinking. More often than not, negative thoughts have been part of our personalities for a long period of time. It usually takes time and effort to change this habit. This is why CBT also covers steps that you can do at home such as learning how you can recognize if you are worried and what it feels like physically and learning relaxation techniques and coping skills to combat panic and anxiety.

Exposure Therapy for Anxiety Disorder

We tend to avoid anxiety because it is rather unpleasant. Among the most common ways people do this is by avoiding certain situations that make them feel anxious.

If you have fear of cockroaches, you may spend time cleaning your home so you can prevent encountering the insect. Or if you feel anxious about speaking in public, you may say no to an important presentation that could lead to your promotion at work. Apart from the factor of inconvenience, the primary issue with avoiding fear is that you may never have the opportunity to challenge them. As a matter of fact, steering clear of the things that you are afraid of could only fortify your fear.

As the name suggests, exposure therapy is a form of CBT that will expose you to certain objects or situations that you are afraid of. The concept is that through a series of exposures, you may feel a growing sense of control over a situation and as a result, your anxiety could decrease.

This is often done in two ways. First, you may confront this in real life. Second, you will be asked by your therapist to think of a scary situation. This form of therapy could be used as a standalone treatment, or it could be done as part of a CBT session.

Systematic Desensitization

Facing your biggest fear head-on could be a traumatic experience, so Exposure Therapy often begins with a scenario that is mildly traumatizing. This process is known as systematic desensitization, which will enable you to gradually face your fears, learn skills to control panic, and build confidence. Take a look at a sample progression below:

How to Face Fear of Heights - Bungee Jumping Exposure
Step 1: Look at photos of popular bungee jumping spots
Step 2: Watch a video of a person doing a bungee jump
Step 3: Find the nearest bungee jumping spot in your area
Step 4: Learn how to properly and safely perform a bungee jump
Step 5: Ask someone to accompany you
Step 6: Go to the spot where you will perform the bungee jump
Step 7: Make sure safety gears are in place
Step 8: Close your eyes and take a deep breath
Step 9: Celebrate success by jumping
Step 10: Repeat some other time

There are three parts in systematic desensitization:

1. Mastering relaxation skills
Your CBT specialist will teach you how to relax through deep breathing or progressive muscle relaxation. You can practice this at home or during the session. When you begin facing your fears, you can use this relaxation strategy to decrease your physical anxiety response (hyperventilating or trembling) and allow you to relax.

2. Create a List
You need to make a list of at least 10 frightening situations that could help you move forward to your ultimate goal. For instance, if your ultimate goal is to overcome your fear of heights, you could begin looking at famous bungee jumping spots and end with actually doing a bungee jump. Every step must be specific as possible with actual measurable goals.

3. Work through the Steps
With the supervision of a CBT specialist, you need to start working on the list. The objective here is to stay in every frightening scenario until your

fear wanes. With this, you will learn that the feelings will not hurt you, and they will tend to go away.

Each time the anxiety gets too overwhelming, you can change to the relaxation technique that you have learned. After relaxing again, you could refocus again to the situation. Through this, you can work through each step until you can complete the list without feeling the bad effects of anxiety.

Other Recommended Therapies for Anxiety Disorder

Aside from CBT, you may also want to explore other recommended therapies that are intended to provide you general stress relief and assist you in achieving good emotional well-being.

Relaxation Techniques

Once regularly performed, relaxation techniques such as visualization, controlled breathing, progressive muscle relaxation, and mindfulness meditation could reduce anxiety and increase relaxation as well as promote healthy emotions.

Exercise

Exercise is a natural anxiety reliever and stress reliever. Based on studies, at least 30 minutes of exercise for 3 to 5 times a week could bring you considerable results in relieving anxiety. In order to attain maximum benefit, try to work out at least one hour of aerobic exercise on most days of the week.

Hypnosis

Hypnosis is often times used in combination with CBT for the treatment of anxiety disorder. While you are in a state of deep relaxation, your therapist can use various therapeutic techniques to help you face your fears and also gain new perspective.

Biofeedback

Through sensors that could measure specific physiological functions like muscle tension, breathing, and heart rate, biofeedback could enable you to learn how you can distinguish the anxiety response of your body and learn ways to control them through specific relaxation techniques.

How to Make Anxiety Therapy Worthwhile

Remember, there is no magical spell or a potion you can drink to make your anxiety vanish away in seconds. The treatment for anxiety disorder will take time and effort. This involves facing your fears instead of staying away from them, so there are times that you may feel worse before you can even feel relief. Nevertheless, you should stick to the treatment plan and follow the advice of your therapist. When you are overwhelmed with the progression of recovery, just remember that therapy for anxiety is most effective for long-term success. You can reap long-lasting rewards as long as you do your part.

It is also possible for you to support your own anxiety therapy through positive choices. This covers everything from your activity level to your social life that could affect anxiety. You can set the platform for success by making a more proactive decision to promote a positive mental outlook, vitality, and relaxation in your daily living.

Live a Healthy Lifestyle

Any physical stress could relieve anxiety and tension, so make certain that you have time for regular exercise. Never use drugs or alcohol to cope with the symptoms of your anxiety, and stay away from stimulants such as nicotine and caffeine that may worsen your anxiety disorder.

Avoid Your Life Stressors

Evaluate your life for stress and explore ways to reduce tension. Stay away from people who could make you anxious, and say no to other obligations. Allow fun and relaxation activities in your daily schedule.

Nurture Your Relationships

Isolation and loneliness could set the stage for anxiety. Reduce your exposure by connecting with people you care. Make certain that you see your friends regularly, volunteer in organizations, and share your concerns and worries with a loved one whom you really care about.

Learn More about Anxiety

To combat anxiety, it is crucial that you fully understand the problem. This is where learning comes in. Reading alone will not treat anxiety disorder, but it could help you in making sure that you get the most of your treatment.

Chapter 11.
CBT and Anger Management

Anger is a natural emotion that we all feel, even though sometimes it can be irrational or unwanted. Psychotherapists refer to anger as a natural, primary emotion that has evolved as our way to survive and protect ourselves from what we consider to be unfair.

Mild anger could arise if we are feeling irritated, stressed, or tired. We usually feel these things when our basic needs as humans such as food, shelter, or sleep are not met or are compromised in some way.

We may feel anger when responding to a threat, criticism, or frustration. But this doesn't mean it is an inappropriate or bad response. People also feel irate by other people's actions, opinions, and beliefs, so anger could also affect our capacity to effectively communicate. This makes us more likely to say or do irrational things.

Being irrational or unreasonable could lead other people around us to feel angry, resentful, or threatened. These can all affect our health as it can elevate our stress levels.

There are instances that anger is a secondary emotion to loneliness, threat, fear, or sadness. It is crucial to try understanding the root cause of your anger at any point in time so the problem can be properly addressed.

You should also take note that anger is not a mere state of mind. It can also trigger physical changes such as hypertension, increased heart rate, and elevated hormones such as adrenaline to prepare our body for the fight or flight response. Because of these physical effects, exposure to anger for a long-time could be damaging to your health and wellbeing.

How We Express Anger

Humans can express anger in different ways. Various forms of anger could affect people in different ways and could manifest to produce various actions and anger manifestations. The most typical signs of anger are both non-verbal and verbal.

It could be obvious that someone feels anger based on what they say or the manner they say it or from the tone of their voice. This natural emotion could also be expressed through body language and other non-verbal cues such as clenching of fists, frowning, staring, trying to look bigger and intimidating. Some people are skilled in internalizing their anger and it could be challenging to spot any physical indication.

By our natural instinct, we often use anger as a way to safeguard our kind or our territory as a response to possible danger or threats. Other reasons could be quite wide-ranging and usually rational and sometimes irrational. Anger that is irrational could mean that it can be difficult for you to manage your anger or even accept the fact that you are angry. CBT can be used as way to properly manage anger.

Five Important Reasons Why You Should Control Anger

Unfortunately, some people resort to violence when they are angry, while others have learned how they control their feelings. While it is normal to be angry, there are several reasons why you must control anger.

1. Anger Can Affect Your Health

Typical health effects of anger may include digestive problems, insomnia, depression, and headache. If a person is always angry, there's a higher chance of hypertension, heart attack, and stroke. In a study published in the Journal of the American College of Cardiology, researchers discovered a connection between hostility and anger to heart conditions. For people who are healthy, heart problems could arise, and for those who are already diagnosed with heart ailments, they could experience a higher risk of heart attack or stroke.

2. Anger Can Affect Relationships
People who are always angry tend to do unreasonable things toward people around them. Usually, words that can hurt feelings are spoken and these could damage relationships beyond repair. That's why you here people giving advice about counting to ten before saying anything in anger.

3. Anger Could Cause You To Lose Focus
When you are always angry at work, it could significantly affect your performance and damage your relationship with your colleagues. It can even cost you your job.

When you are always angry at home, you will miss the chance to spend quality time with your family.

4. You Will Look Older
A person who always frowns will look older, lethargic, and exude a negative aura. Meanwhile, a person who always smiles will seem youthful, energetic, and open.

5. Anger Will Affect Your Personal Image
If you are always angry, it can negatively affect your image as an individual. The last thing you like is to be tagged by your coworkers, friends, and family as a person who is toxic and not fun to be around. Soon, you will notice that they find always find ways to avoid you.

It is true that anger is a normal emotion, but if not controlled, it can affect your social life, your physical health, and your mental state. However, anger must also not be suppressed as too much repression may trigger depression. One way to manage anger is through CBT.

Seven Steps in Anger Management through CBT

Failure to meet expectations could result in anger. When we are expecting people around us to be fair and they are not, we usually feel angry. When we expect our colleagues to respect us, and they don't, we tend to get angry.

Every time that there is a gap between our expectations and the actual things that are happening, anger could come in and fill this gap. Every time someone is breaking the rules we have set, behaves against our expectations, or fails to comply with an agreement, we are presented with the option to be angry. We can give in to the emotion or we can choose to suppress it. The expression of our anger depends on our choice.

Through CBT, you can effectively manage your anger, and the first step in this process is to recognize your choice. There are many things that are beyond our control - our emotions, physical sensations, temptations, other people, the past, the future, or even as simple as the weather. But the key in anger management is to be aware of our capacity to choose how we respond to anger trigger points.

We can choose what we want to do within the context of sensations, emotions, or thoughts. We can choose how we can interact with the people around us, what we learn from our past, and how we respond to the weather. Basically, we can also choose if we want to concentrate on things that are beyond our control, or those that we can control.

An effective strategy in recognizing this decision is to weigh down the benefits and the cost of responding to anger. Try to imagine someone who can handle a strong emotion in a manner that you really admire and respect. Let's call him John. What character traits can you think of to describe John? Forgiving? Controlled? Easy-going? Calm? Cool? Assertive? Regardless of the word you choose, write this down. Just be sure to choose someone whose character you really admire and respect. After this, try to answer the four questions below:

What are the advantages of emulating John?
What are the disadvantages of anger?
What are the costs of anger?
What are the benefits of being like John?

Then, find out if the cost of anger outweighs the benefits. Are they on the same level? Is the cost of anger heavier than its benefits?

Use a specific number to describe the cost-benefit analysis: 100 to 0, 90 to 10, 80 to 20, 70 to 30, 60 to 40, 55 to 45, 50 to 50? Repeat these steps with the benefits and costs of following the style of John:

Advantages of Anger

- Could be constructive
- Allows expression of emotion
- Provides a boost

Weight: 20

Disadvantages of Anger

- It can make the situation a lot worse
- It can affect my physical health
- It can hurt me physically and emotionally
- It could be harmful to me and the people around me

Weight: 80

Benefits of Being Like John

- I will not have the burden of holding a grudge
- I can respond in a constructive manner

- I can move on
- It's important in achieving happiness
- I don't reside in anger

Weight: 60

Cost of Being Like John
- People will not care how things could affect me
- People will probably still do things that annoy me
- They may step all over me

Weight: 30

Remember, the cost of anger is actually the cost of aggression. Even though it can be difficult to control our anger, we still have complete control over what we can do with this emotion.

We may choose to be passive, aggressive, angry-assertive, or passive-aggressive. It all boils down to our preference. Feeling anger can easily fast-track our response to our emotion and can present an illusion that we don't have any choice. Yet we have to reshape our lives by considering how we decide to deal with our anger.

Step 1 - Recognize that a rule violation has occurred

In the CBT context of anger management, the first step is the recognition of a rule violation. We have specific rules as well as expectations that we follow for our personal behavior. We also use these rules to expect how people around us should behave. Hence, we can also feel the heaviness of the rules set by other people. The outcome is pressure, guilt, and anger. Are you familiar with the statements below?

I should have complete control over this situation.
He has the audacity to show his face to me?
That kid should listen to me!
My mom should support me on this.

Many people say these things out loud or internally. These are just some of the statements that indicate expectations. The problem is, in real life, people don't always behave according to our expectations. In fact, people could be a stumbling block for us -- people don't listen to us, and we may not have any control as to the outcomes of our actions.

It is crucial that we learn how to accept the given situation: accept reality instead of denying it or wishing it doesn't exist. While we have complete control over our choices, the truth is that we also have minimal control over other people.

Then, we can follow a way that is in accordance with our personal core values. The challenge is getting to know these specific values. We can identify our values depending on what engages us, disappoints us, and angers us. In particular, we should pinpoint the positive values that underlie our rule.

For example:
If a person says something like *"That kid should learn how to listen"*, it indicates that he puts a premium on cooperation, understanding, and/or communication.

If a person says something like *"He should learn how to work with me"*, it could imply that he places importance on progress, respect, and freedom.

We don't have control if other people respond with respect to our values. We can only have control if we do.

It's also crucial to act on your values. Try to think of what you want for the long-term and the specific steps you can take in this direction.

People often ignore our rules and interfere with our lives. So how can you respond constructively if you face a similar situation? You can respond with fairness, truth, and respect. Try to become the solution instead of being part of the problem.

Step 2 - Recognize the pain points

Next, we need to assess our pain points when people violate our rules. Some of these are rules that comprise the core of our *self*, while others are on the sidelines.

For instance, once we feel anger, you can ask yourself: *what is really causing your pain?* After all, anger is often caused by things or people that we deem unjust and therefore objectionable or unpleasant. This may reflect a general concept of our belief in ourselves and in other people around us.

Some people answer the question this way:

- I feel weak in this situation.
- I feel like a victim in this.
- He is insensitive and rude.

One thing that can really be painful is if we fail to change the behavior of other people. Keep in mind that there's no actual proof that we must change people who should be accountable for their own opinions, attitudes, behaviors, and beliefs.

Step 3 - Reflect on your response

Next, reflect on how you can constructively respond to your angry thoughts. There's a big difference between reactive and reflective responses. For example:

Reactive: *What an idiot!*
Reflective: *He's just a human being who makes mistakes.*

Reactive: *How rude!*
Reflective: *Maybe he is going through something that I don't know about.*

Step 4 - Respond to Anger

The next step involves the actual response to anger. You can work around anger through different relaxation techniques such as listening to music, playing a musical instrument, visualization, or mindfulness meditation.

Meanwhile, other people can also redefine anger itself by considering anger as an energy that can solve a problem. You can use anger to do the right thing in the name of morals, principles, and values that are important to us.

Anger can be a problem if we are using it to violate our principles. It can become part of the problem if we are using it to treat the people around us in ways that we find disgusting. It can become a problem if we use it to fuel aggression or hypocrisy. But just as Abraham Lincoln was disgusted at slavery, we could use anger as a tool for a constructive action that is based on our principles.

Step 5 - Disengage

Once we learn how to properly respond to anger, we need to take a closer look at common beliefs that usually convert anger to aggression. More often than not, these are excuses and rationalizations that could support harmful behavior:

- Damn it! I have valid reasons to be angry!
- I don't care. He crossed the line!
- She deserves to be slapped for saying those words to me!

We should take note that these ideas are deceptive. They deceive us into setting aside our principles and instead give in to blame, demands, sarcasm, and threats. We must be reminded of the benefits of pursuing grace, empathy, understanding, and patience as well as the costs of giving in to anger.

Step 6 - Evaluate dysfunctional behaviors

Responding to anger and choosing to disengage is not the last step in using CBT for anger management. We also need to take a closer look at particular behaviors, which may arise. Some people succumb to the desire to lash out -- they respond aggressively and set aside other people's welfare.

But we can also react in a different manner – you can prevent feeding your anger. You can do this by nurturing your empathy. Try to consider their viewpoints. Just imagine what they may feel or think, and try to really see things from their eyes. This could help in reducing your anger, reducing other people's anger and increasing the chances that people will listen to us. It could even boost the chances of being able to participate in a more reasonable conversation.

Step 7 - Assess the results

Finally, we need to try controlling guilt and resentment. Some people have the tendency to view each episode of anger as a setback or a failure. However, every instance of anger could be used as a way to become successful. The key is to assess and intervene with the things that could trigger our anger. When we become more familiar with this practice, we can experience less intense anger arousal.

The seven steps in CBT anger management signify specific points that we can use to stop anger. More often than not, we are more inclined to view anger as urgent and so we may be slow to control this valid human emotion. Another perspective is to view anger as a potential energy that could arise if our expectations don't meet reality. This is the energy to manage this gap, and we really need to manage our choices.

Managing anger through specific steps could allow us to be in control of the situation, and provide us more options for prevention and intervention.

Chapter 12.
How to Overcome Bad Habits through CBT

Psychologists refer to habits as our brain's way to autopilot tasks. Habits help us prepare for work, find the way to our workplace, and go home without the need to reinvent the wheel every day. It can save us time and energy, unless the habit is not contributing to our growth as humans – these harmful habits include eating popcorn at midnight or biting your nails.

How Habits Form

To take a closer look why some habits could be difficult to change, psychologists from the University of California conducted tests with mice and discovered that the circuits of the brain responsible for our goals and habits formation are competing against each other in the part of the brain that makes decisions.

According to Christina Gremel, a researcher from University of California in San Diego, neurochemicals known as endocannabinoids permit habit to take over by acting as a type of brake on the circuit of the brain that is goal directed. Our body naturally produces endocannabinoids with receptors scattered throughout our brain and body. This process is involved in different physiological processes like memory, mood, pain sensation, and appetite.

Initial studies also reveal that there is a specific part of the brain that transmits goal-directed messages. This is known as the orbitofrontal cortex (OFC). During experiments, when the researchers added the intensity of neurons in this area through optogenetics - a lab technique that uses flashes of light, the goal-directed actions also intensified. And when the researchers decreased the intensity of the OFC using the same technique, the lab mice acted on their formed habit.

There should be a good balance between goal-directed and habitual actions with everyday task management and functioning. Through our habits, we can be more efficient and fast in our daily tasks. But we also experience changing habits and require the ability to break the habits and do a goal-directed action that is based on updated information.

For example, when we need to go to a workplace for the first time, our brain shifts from habit to goal-oriented action. The decision to change a habit also depends on the goal-directed action right from the start. Mice that are healthy had no problem shifting from one action to another. However, psychologists suggest that people who are suffering from mental disorders such as substance addiction or obsessive-compulsive disorder could have physical impediments that inhibit the goal-directed behavior. One way to change bad habits is through CBT.

Six Steps to Break Bad Habits through Cognitive Behavioral Therapy

Remember, habits are actually behaviors that we have learned over time. Hence, we can unlearn these habits by becoming aware of them and being persistent to change our ways.

The more we give in to our habits, the more they become strong and entrenched in our system. But each time we try to do something that is different from our habits, they will be weaker and the new behavior will eventually become stronger as you practice them. CBT offers a step-by-step approach to breaking bad habits:

Step 1 - Decide to Make the Decision Today

The very first step in breaking your habit is to make the decision to do something about your bad habit. It is crucial to make the decision today -

not tomorrow as it will reinforce within you the determination to change. Once you thought about the damages brought by the habit, you are more driven to do something about it.

Moreover, it is also crucial to focus on the benefits you can obtain when you are successful in breaking the habit. Think about the worst case scenario of going on with the habit and this could drive you to act on it. You may even resolve to quit the habit right at this first step. There are people who have developed the bad habit of checking their email every five minutes to the point that it has become counterproductive. When you become more aware of why you need to change this habit, it becomes easier to change.

Step 2 - Practice Mindfulness

To put a stop to a bad habit, you must first become aware and accept the fact that your habit is detrimental to yourself as a person. You also need to accept the reality that only you could stop it. It is essential that you are aware of the disadvantages of sticking to your bad habit.

For instance, if you are constantly binge-watching Netflix even on a work night, you need to think about the circumstances that drive you to spend countless hours to watching shows that may not be contributing to your well-being. How do you feel when you wake up in the morning after a night of watching a whole season?

It is crucial to keep track of your habit and get to know the circumstances and frequency when you usually engage in these habits. For example, if you bite your nails, do you do it when you are at home or at work? Also, take note of your emotion when you do this habit.

Carefully study your habit at least weekly. By doing this, you can see an emerging trend and you can discover the antecedents of the behavior.

Identify the things that could trigger your habit. What are the environmental triggers that drive you to plunge into your bad habit? By being mindful of your bad habits, the frequency declines, which is an important step in making the much-needed change.

You will find a detailed discussion on Mindfulness in the next chapter, as well as some exercises that could help you become more mindful.

Step 3 - Use CBT Strategies to Change the Habit

Take note that the fundamental concept in CBT revolves around our thoughts, our emotions, and our behavior. The way we think will affect the way we feel and act. Hence, CBT is an effective form of treatment for stopping bad habits.

One effective CBT strategy in dealing with bad habits is the basic STOP technique. Once you become aware that you are doing a bad habit, you need to stop it right away by literally saying STOP to yourself. Some people find it helpful to write the word STOP on a piece of paper and display it near their work area or somewhere that is easily seen so they are reminded to stop their bad habit right away.

It is also ideal to seek support from a family, friend, or a colleague at work who could observe you and tell you when you are in your bad habit again. Just keep track of your habit, and try to reward yourself for breaking the bad habit.

Also, remember that this is not supposed to be easy. Don't be discouraged even if you feel that you are not successful. It's possible that your habits may even become worse during the early stages. This could be because you are now trying to monitor something that you were used to do automatically. It is also possible that mindfulness triggers more tension and anxiety and the frequency is thus increased. Never give up as this phase will not last long.

Step 4 - Find New Alternatives to Your Bad Habit

If your bad habit involves using your hand, you can try keeping your hands occupied through an alternative activity, so that it will stop you from nail biting or hair pulling. Playing with a stress ball could help.

Women also use manicure products or hand cream to resolve their nail-biting habits, while some who habitually rub their eyes wear makeup so they are discouraged to do the habit. Be sure that you are aware of the specific types of feelings that trigger you to do the bad habits.

If you know that it is boredom, worry, anxiety, or tension, then try doing something about this specific emotional trigger. When you have a bad habit of gossiping, then try to become more mindful if you are sharing a story that is untrue or not intended to be shared.

If you tend to be messy with your room, try to develop habits such as wiping down counters after you pour yourself some milk or make dinner.

Step 5 - Be Persistent and Monitor Your Progress

Persistency and consistency are two crucial factors to break a bad habit. You will never achieve your goal of changing your ways if you work hard for the first week only to dwindle your determination after several days. You should persistently on the go and keep track of your habits.

Breaking a bad habit, especially if you have had it years already, may never be easy. It is just natural to feel the urge to just give up. However, you must instill in your mind that giving up will not help you. Try focusing on the reward for all your hard work - better health, becoming more productive, or earning more money. Maintain your habit journal and be mindful of the moments when you catch yourself doing the habit again.

Step 6 - Cope With Setbacks

There is no magical formula that you can follow or a potion you can drink to completely remove a bad habit. Behaviors that you have learned for many years have the tendency to pop their ugly heads until you have completely break them off. Because habits are fairly automatic, they could re-emerge anytime. Hence, you must develop the mindfulness (more on this in later chapters) and willpower to break these habits completely to avoid re-emergence. When you experience some lapses, try to find out why it has happened and continue making your efforts to be successful. The more your work on it, the higher the chance of your habit to break off.

It is also helpful if you start changing smaller bad habits (going back to sleep after the alarm sounds off, nail biting) so you can progress with major bad habits (procrastination, lying, taking too much debt). Once you have dealt with your smaller bad habits, you will be more inclined to take bigger challenges head-on.

Through CBT, you can effectively break the habit, and you can have a better chance to reduce your anxiety, increase your self-confidence, and live a better life. Bad habits are the precursor to addiction such as drug abuse, drinking, or smoking. Changing your bad habits will allow you to take care of yourself and your family.

It is crucial to be mindful of your bad habits such as tapping, nail biting, facial grimaces, twitching, repetitive mannerisms, and obsessional thinking. Most of these bad habits are caused by timidity, passivity, repressed anger, unresolved conflict, depression, cumulative stress, and internal tension.

You can address bad habits through CBT, through the steps we have discussed above. When you experience some of the feelings that we have discussed in this book, it is best to seek professional advice so you can properly address unresolved feelings. CBT is a proven effective treatment and engaging in mindfulness can also help you relieve anxiety and tension.

Chapter 13.
Mindfulness

Mindfulness is a basic technique in psychotherapy that is used to mainly treat anxiety, anger, depression, and other psychological problems. While it has its roots in the mysticism of the Eastern cultures, science has already studied the subject a great deal and psychotherapists even recommend mindfulness meditation for individuals who are suffering from certain mental health problems. Developing mindfulness is a crucial part of CBT, as well as DBT and ACT. In fact, it is one of the four skills modules in DBT.

Basically, mindfulness is the state of our mind that can be achieved by focusing our awareness on what is happening at the present. It also involves the calm acceptance of our feelings, sensations, and thoughts.

The challenge of focusing in the present could be trivial for some, but this is actually easier said than done. Our mind could wander away, we lose touch with the present moment, and we could even be absorbed into obsessive thoughts about the things that have happened in the past or worrying about the future. But regardless of how far away our mind drifts away from the present, we can use mindfulness to immediately get us back to what we are presently doing or feeling.

Even though it is natural for us to be mindful anytime we want, we can cultivate it through effective ACT techniques that you will learn later on.

Mindfulness is usually linked with meditation. While meditation is an effective way to achieve mindfulness, there's more to it. Mindfulness is a form of being present, which you can use any time. It is a form of consciousness that you can achieve if you intentionally focus on the present moment without any judgment.

Elements of mindfulness

Attention and attitude are the two primary elements of mindfulness.

Attention

Many of us are suffering from what is known as monkey mind, wherein the mind behaves like a monkey swinging from one branch to another. Our mind could swing away there and back again, and we usually don't have any idea how we end up thinking about something.

The monkey mind usually dwells in the past, ruminating what has happened or what you think must have happened if you have acted differently. It also swings away to the future being anxious about what could happen. Nourishing the monkey mind will steal away the experience of the present moment.

Remember, mindfulness is focusing your attention on what is happening now.

Attitude

Suspending judgment and kindness are the basic tenets of mindfulness. Hence, a genuinely mindful person knows how to accept the reality and doesn't engage in arguing with it. This may seem an easy task, but once you begin practicing mindfulness, you will be aware how frequently we judge ourselves and our thoughts.

Here are some examples of sentences used in judgment of ourselves and others:

- I'm not good at this task.
- My shirt looks lame.

- I don't like my home.
- I really don't like my neighbor.
- What a grumpy waitress.

Mindfulness is also the art of calming our inner judge. It allows us to erase our internal expectations and become more embracing of how things are in the present moment. But take note that this doesn't mean you don't need to make necessary changes, and you will just allow everything to happen.

Remember, you are only suspending your judgment, so you can have more time to think about the situation and do something about it. The main difference is that you can make changes from the ideal state of your mind for change and not during times that you are influenced by tension or stress.

Moreover, mindfulness will allow you to be more compassionate with yourself, more embracing of your experience, and more caring of the people around you. It will also allow you to be more patient and non-judgmental if you make some lapses. As you practice mindfulness, you can reshape your brain to become kinder and more compassionate.

How Mindfulness Can Reshape Your Brain

In the past, people believed that the human brain can only be developed in a certain level, usually from early childhood to adolescence. But various studies reveal that our brain has the capacity to reorganize itself through forming neural connections. This is known as neuroplasticity and it has no virtually no limit.

Neuroscientists shattered the old belief that the human brain is an unchanging, static organ. They discovered that despite of age, disease, or injury, the human brain can compensate for any damage by restructuring itself. To put it simply, our brain is capable of repairing itself.

More studies also support the idea that mindfulness can significantly help in the brain's development. It specifically helps in the process of neuroplasticity. It is really amazing to know that we can change our emotions, feelings, and thought processes through neuroplasticity and mindfulness.

There are three major studies that show how mindfulness can rewire the human brain through neuroplasticity.

Mindfulness Can Improve Memory, Learning, and Other Cognitive Functions

Even though mindfulness meditation is linked with a sense of physical relaxation and calmness, practitioners claim that the practice can also help in learning and memory.

Sara Lazar, a professor at Harvard University Medical School pioneered an 8-week meditation program that primarily uses mindfulness. With her team of researchers from Massachusetts General Hospital, she conducted the program to explore the connection between mindfulness and the improvement of cognitive functions.

The program was composed of weekly meditation sessions as well as audio recordings for the 16 volunteers who practiced meditation alone. On average, the participants practiced meditation for around 27 minutes. The underlying concept of the mindfulness meditation for the research was on achieving a state of mind in which the participants will suspend their judgment and just focus on feeling sensations.

Later on, the team used Magnetic Resonance Imaging (MRI) to capture images of the brain structure of the participants. A group of individuals who were not meditating (the control group) were also asked for MRI scan.

The researchers were amazed by the result. Primarily, the study participants revealed that they experienced significant cognitive advantages that were proven in their responses in the mindfulness survey. On top of that, the researchers also noted measurable physical differences in the density of the gray matter as supported by MRI scan.

- The gray-matter density in the amygdala, the area of the brain responsible for stress and anxiety was decreased.
- There were significant changes in the brain areas responsible for self-awareness, introspection, and compassion
- The gray-matter density in the hippocampus, the part of the brain responsible for memory and learning was increased.

This Harvard study reveals that the brain's neuroplasticity, and through practicing meditation, we can play an active role in the development of our brain. It is exciting to know that we can do something every day to improve our quality of life and general well-being.

Mindfulness Can Help Combat Depression

Millions of people around the world are suffering from depression. For example, in the US, there are about 19 million people who are seeking medication to combat depression. This is around 10% of the whole US population.

Dr. Zindel Segal, a Psychiatry Professor at the University of Toronto used a research grant from MacArthur Foundation to explore the advantages of mindfulness towards alleviating depression. The research that was mainly focused on the administration of Mindfulness Based Stress Reduction session was considered a success that he conducted a follow up research to study the effectiveness of mindfulness meditation to patients afflicted by depression. This has resulted in the establishment of Mindfulness Based Cognitive Therapy or MBCT.

The study involved patients who are suffering from depression, with 8 out of 10 experiencing at least three episodes of depression. Meanwhile, around 30% of the study participants who experienced at least three episodes of depression had not relapsed for more than a year in comparison to those who followed a prescribed therapy (mainly through antidepressants).

The result was astounding that it has become a precursor of several research sponsored by the Oxford and Cambridge University in the United Kingdom, with both studies generating similar outcomes. The research has significantly proved valuable in using mindfulness meditation as an effective and healthier alternative to medication in the UK that has convinced mental health practitioners to prescribe mindfulness meditation to their patients.

Mindfulness meditation and research studies on MBCT are gradually taking a foothold within medical and scientific circles in the US and other parts of the globe.

Mindfulness Can Help in Stress Relief

A study conducted at the Carnegie Mellon University has revealed that the practice of mindfulness, even for 25 minutes a day, can alleviate stress. The study, led by Prof. David Creswell, involved 66 participants with ages between 18 and 30 years.

One group of study subjects was asked to undergo a short meditation session composed of 25 minutes mindfulness session for three days. This group was asked to do some exercises that are designed to get them to concentrate on breathing while turning their focus to the present moment. The second group used the same time to assess poetry readings to improve their problem-solving skills.

During the evaluation phase, all the study participants were asked to complete math and speech tasks in front of evaluators who were asked to look stern. All participants reported their stress levels increased and were asked for saliva samples to measure the levels of the stress hormone cortisol.

The group who was asked to practice mindfulness meditation for at least 25 minutes for three days reported less stress from the provided task, showing that practicing mindfulness even in the short term could increase the body's ability to handle stress.

It is interesting to take note that the same group showed higher levels of the stress hormone, which was not expected by the researchers.

The research concluded that when participants learn mindfulness meditation, they have to actively work on the process - particularly in a stressful situation. The cognitive task may feel less stressful for the individual, despite of elevated cortisol level.

The team is now focusing on automating the mindfulness sessions to make it less stressful while reducing the cortisol levels. But it is clear that even in initial phases, a short-term practice of meditation can show a great deal in relieving stress.

Other Benefits of Mindfulness

Aside from the benefits described above, mindfulness meditation provides great benefits for our emotional, mental, and physical health.

Emotional Benefits

Mindfulness allows us to be more compassionate. Those who practice mindfulness meditation show changes in specific areas of the brain that are associated with empathy.

Mindfulness meditation decreases our reactivity to our emotions. A study conducted in the Massachusetts General Hospital reveals that mindfulness reduces the size of the amygdala, which is responsible for fear, anxiety, and aggression.

Mindfulness meditation can help us to avoid negative thoughts, which our brain usually resort to once they are left on its own.

In 2007, a study was conducted among students who were taught meditation strategies. It revealed that mindfulness helped the students increase their focus, and decrease self-doubt, anxiety, and depression. There was also a notable decrease in suspensions and absenteeism in schools where mindfulness sessions are encouraged.

Mindfulness is also now used to ease the symptoms of anxiety and depression. Many psychotherapists are now prescribing mindfulness meditation for their patients who are suffering from depressive episodes.

Mental Health Benefits
A study published in the Journal of Psychological Science reveals that students who practiced meditation before taking an exam got better results compared to students who did not. The study discovered a link between mindfulness and better cognitive function.

Mindfulness increases the activity in the anterior cingulate, which is a part of the brain that is responsible for memory, learning, and emotional regulation. It also increases activity in the prefrontal cortex that is responsible for judgment and planning.

Mindfulness is linked to improved concentration and longer attention span.

Mindfulness meditation also increases the brain's neural connections and has been proven to fortify myelin, which is the protective tissue that surrounds the neurons responsible for transmitting signals in the brain.

Physical Benefits

Deep breathing can deactivate our sympathetic nervous system which is responsible for our fight or flight response. It also activates the parasympathetic nervous system that is responsible for our rest and digest mode.

Mindfulness decreases the cortisol level of the body. This stress hormone increases levels of stress and encourages hypertension.

In one study, participants who practiced mindfulness meditation reduced their risk for heart attack by more than five years and also reduced their blood pressure.

Mindfulness allows our mind to be aware of what we eat, and has been used for weight loss programs.

Mindfulness is also responsible for increasing telomerase, which is believed to help in the decrease of cell damage.

Mindfulness meditation has been shown to increase the production of antibodies that combat flu virus. This shows that meditation can help us boost our immune system.

What Does Mindfulness Truly Mean?

Mindfulness means being aware of the things happening right this very moment in both our immediate surroundings, and in ourselves — our thoughts, our emotions, our physical sensations, and our behaviors. The purpose of this awareness is to prevent us from being controlled by these events. This awareness must also be nonjudgmental and passing, that is, we focus only on the facts and accept them, avoiding our own evaluations or opinions, and then we let them go.

Suppose your boss has severely criticized you about the work you've done. You know that you do not deserve it -- both the criticism and the way it was delivered, and so you become very angry.

However, instead of letting your emotions dictate your response, you take a step back and mindfully think about the situation, and say to yourself something like this, "My boss is under a lot of pressure right now, cranky and easily angered. His criticism of me was unfair. I did not deserve it, and so I got furious." And then you move on.

The Three States of Mind

There are different psychotherapy skills associated with mindfulness, and the above example is only one application of them. Those who are learning these skills undergo exercises, like meditation and mindful walking. But from this example alone we can now easily understand and appreciate the benefits of mindfulness.

There is what is called the Wise Mind, which is one of the three states of our mind. It is the balance between our Reasonable Mind (when we act and behave based solely on facts and reason) and Emotion Mind (when our thoughts and actions are dictated by our feelings). When we are using our wise mind — the wisdom in each one of us — we recognize and acknowledge our feelings, but we respond to them rationally.

Wise Mind, or the practice of using our wisdom, is actually the first of mindfulness skills. As illustrated above, mindfulness helps us manage and control ourselves well, especially in sudden and emotionally-intense situations, where we are more likely to react with our emotion mind. This one benefit alone has many positive consequences in the long run — better relationships, better self-esteem and better self-respect, better responses to unexpected crises, and lesser symptoms of anxiety and depression.

More important, with being mindful, we also get to experience life more fully.

Mindfulness skills also train our minds, and so we get the added benefits of improved memory, sharper focus, and faster mental processing. Our anxiety is also reduced and we gain more control of our thoughts.

Core Mindfulness Skills

And so, what exactly are these mindfulness skills? They are divided into three groups: Wise Mind, the "what" skills, and the "how" skills.

Wise Mind
As explained above, this is the middle state between our Reasonable Mind and Emotion Mind, where we recognize both our reason and emotions, and act accordingly.

The "What" Skills
These skills are in answer to the question, "What are the things you must do to practice mindfulness?" The answers are (1) to observe, (2) to describe, and (3) to participate.

Observe.
To observe is nothing more than to experience and be aware of our surroundings, our thoughts, our feelings, and the sensations we're receiving. This is stepping back and looking at ourselves, especially for reorientation when we are too much preoccupied with our problems.

Describe.
To describe is to put words on our present experiences — acknowledging what we feel, think, or do — and using only the facts to do it, without our own opinions. For example, we say to ourselves, "My stomach feels hungry," or "I'm thinking about my mother." Doing this lessens distraction and helps our focus.

Participate.
To participate is to give ourselves fully to what we are doing at the moment (eating, talking, or feeling satisfied). We forget ourselves in it, and we act spontaneously.

The "How" Skills

These skills, on the other hand, answer the question, "How are you going to practice mindfulness?" The answers are: (1) non-judgmentally, (2) one-mindfully, and (3) effectively.

Non-judgmentally. A nonjudgmental stance is seeing only the facts without evaluating, and without personal opinion. We accept each moment as it is, including our circumstances and what we see in ourselves: our thoughts, our feelings, our values, etc.

One-mindfully. Practicing mindfulness one-mindfully is doing only one thing at a time, and giving it all of our attention — whether it be dancing, walking, sitting, talking, thinking. This is about maintaining our focus, and increasing our concentration.

Effectively. Practicing mindfulness effectively is keeping our goals in our mind, and doing what is needed to accomplish them. We do our best, and we do not let our emotions get in the way.

These core mindfulness skills are central to Dialectical Behavior Therapy, and they support all the other skills. They are called "core" mindfulness skills because there are a few other skills or perspectives on mindfulness that are less commonly practiced. We will no longer talk about them, but among these other perspectives is one taken from a spiritual point of view, designed for those who need further help in mindfulness in light of their spirituality.

Mindfulness Exercises

Now that we know the skills, it is time to apply them to exercises so that we can see them in action. The following are some mindfulness exercises, a small sampling from the wealth of exercises that have already been developed for DBT.

Meditation

To observe the present moment — in a nonjudgmental way — is the purpose of meditation.

To practice meditation, find a quiet place where you won't be disturbed. The goal is a daily meditation of at least 30 minutes. For beginners, 10 minutes is advised.

Sit on a chair or on a cushion on the floor. Sit with your back comfortably straight, with your arms on your side, and your palms on the top of your thighs.

Then bring your attention to your breathing — pay close attention to your inhalation, exhalation, and the sounds they make. Try to do this for the entire duration. Your breathing is what you are using to ground yourself to this present moment.

However, your mind will soon wander, and that is alright. Simply acknowledge your thoughts without judgment, and then return your attention to your breathing.

You may also experience some uneasy feelings while meditating, and that is alright too. Again, simply acknowledge your feelings without judgment, and then return your attention to your breathing.

Do these, again and again, always returning to your breathing whenever you are distracted until the time is up.

Mindful walking

Mindful walking is simply practicing mindfulness while walking, to observe one's own physical body and the surroundings.

First, take note of how your body moves and how it feels as you take your steps. Notice the pressure on your feet, and the aches in your joints if there are any. Notice the increased rate of your heartbeat.

Then, expand your awareness to what is around you. What do you see? What do you hear? What do you smell? Do you feel the wind or the heat of the sun in your skin?

Five senses

This is about using your five senses to observe your present moment. Notice at least one thing that you see, or feel, or hear, or smell, or taste.

Mindful Breathing

You can do this mindfulness exercise sitting down or standing. If the time and place allow you to sit in a lotus position, do it, if not, there's no problem. You just need to ensure that you are focused on your breathing for at least 60 seconds.

Begin by slowly breathing in and breathing out. One cycle of breathing must last for about six seconds.

Remember to inhale through your nose and exhale through your mouth. Allowing your breathing to flow without any struggle.

While doing this exercise, you should make sure that you can let go of your thoughts. Also, learn to let go of the things that you have to complete today or the pending projects that require your attention. Let your thoughts flow of their own way and focus on your breathing.

Be aware of your breathing, concentrating your consciousness as air enters your body and give your life.

Mindful Listening

This mindfulness exercise is intended to develop our sense of hearing in a non-judgmental manner. This is also effective in training our brain to be less distracted by the effects of preconceptions and previous experiences.

Majority of what we feel is affected by our previous experiences. For instance, we hate a specific song because it triggers bad memories or another moment in your life when you really felt bad.

Mindful listening is designed to allow you to listen to neutral sounds and music, with a present consciousness that is not blocked by any preconception.

Choose music or a soundtrack that you are not really familiar with. Perhaps, you have something in your playlist that you have never listened to, or you may choose to turn on the radio to find a music that you can listen to.

Close your eyes and plug in your earphones.

The objective is to suspend your judgment of any music you hear - its genre, artist, or title. Rather, don't prejudge the label and try to go with the flow of music for the whole time.

Let yourself discover the music, despite the fact that you may not like it at first. Let go of your judgment and allow your consciousness to be with the sound.

Navigate the sound waves by discerning the vibe of every musical instrument used in the music. Try to separate every sound in your mind and assess each.

Also be aware of the vocals - its tone and range. If the music has several voices, try to separate them as you did with the musical instrument.

The goal here is to listen mindfully, to become completely entwined with the music without any judgment or preconception of the music, genre, or artist. This exercise requires you to listen and not to think.

Mindful Observation

This mindfulness exercise is one of the easiest to do but also among the most powerful because it will allow you to appreciate the simpler aspects of your surroundings.

This is intended to reconnect us with the beauty of our environment, which is something that we often ignore when we are driving to work or even walking in the park.

- Select a natural object that you can easily focus on for a couple of minutes. This can be the moon, the clouds, an insect, or a tree.
- Try not to do anything except to observe the thing you have chosen to focus on. Just relax and try to focus on the object as much as your mind allows.
- Look at the object and try to observe its visual aspects. Let your consciousness be consumed by the presence of the object.
- Let yourself be connected with the object's purpose and energy within the natural environment.

Mindful Awareness

This mindfulness exercise is intended to develop our elevated consciousness and appreciation of simple everyday tasks as well as the outcomes they achieve. Consider something that you do every day that you usually take for granted, such as brushing your teeth, for instance.

Right from the moment that you grab your toothbrush, stop for a few moments and be mindful of your presence, your feelings for that moment, and what that action is doing for you.

Likewise, when you open the door before you go out and face the world, take a few moments to be still and appreciate the design of your gateway to the rest of the world.

However, these things don't necessarily have to be physical ones. For instance, every time you feel sadness, you may opt to take a few moments to stop, identify the thought as harmful, accept the fact that human beings get sad, and then move forward -- let go of the negativity.

It can even be something very little, like every time you see a flower on your way to work, take the moment to stop and appreciate how fortunate you are to behold such a visual delight.

Select a touchpoint that really resonates with you today and rather than going through your everyday tasks like a robot, take a few moments to step back and develop purposeful consciousness of what you are currently doing as well as the gifts that these actions will generate for your life.

Mindful Appreciation

In this mindfulness exercise, you will be observing five things in your day that you often ignore. These things could be people, events, or objects. This is really on your call. By the end of the day, write down the list of five things that you have noticed throughout the day.

The goal of this exercise is to basically show your gratitude and appreciation of the things that may seem insignificant in life- the things that also play their role in our human existence, but we often ignore because we focus way too much on the "bigger and more important" things in life.

There are so many of these little things that we barely notice. There's the clean water that nourishes your body, the cab driver that takes you to your workplace, your computer that allows you to be productive, your tongue that allows you to savor that delicious lunch you had.

However, have you ever taken just a few moments to pause and think about your connection to these things and how they play a role in your life?

- Have you ever step back and observe their more intricate, finer details?
- Have you ever wondered what your life will be if these things are not present?
- Have you ever properly appreciated how these things provide you advantage in your life and the people you care?
- Do you really know how these things really work or how they came into existence?

After identifying these five things, try to know everything you can about their purpose and creation. That's how you can genuinely appreciate the way that they are supporting your life.

Mindful Immersion

Mindful immersion is an exercise that will help you develop satisfaction in the present moment and let go of the persistent worrying about what the future may bring.

Instead of anxiously wanting to complete our daily work so we can get on to the next item in the list, we can take the task and completely experience it. For instance, if you need to wash the dishes, focus on the specific details of the activity. Instead of treating this as a common household chore, you can choose to develop a completely new experience by taking a closer look at each aspect of your action.

Feel the rush of water when washing down the plates. Is it cold water? Is it warm water? How does the running water feel on your hands as you do the dishes? Be aware of the movement you use in scrubbing off grease.

The concept is to be creative and find new experiences for a task that is quite monotonous and very common. Rather than struggling through and persistently thinking about completing the task, be conscious of each step and completely immerse yourself in the process. Choose to take the task beyond a routine by aligning yourself with it mentally and physically – and even spiritually, if you're the spiritual kind.

Mindfulness Is For Anyone

You have now learned what mindfulness is, its benefits, the skills associated with it, and the exercises to boost yours. You will need it not just in CBT but also in DBT and ACT, as you'll see in the following chapters.

Without a doubt, becoming more mindful and learning these skills are very useful and rewarding. It is not just a treatment option for those who are afflicted with a mental disorder. Learning to act wisely despite our irrational feelings and being more observant of ourselves and the things around us, are sure to bring us more happiness and contentment in this life. Nurturing our ability to be aware of every moment in our life is a beneficial practice that can help us better manage the negative feelings and thoughts that may cause us anxiety and stress in our lives.

Through regular practice of mindfulness exercises, you will not easily succumb to bad habits and become influenced by fear of the future and the negative experiences of your past. You can finally develop your ability to set your mind in the present and manage the challenges of life in an assertive yet calm manner.

You can in turn reshape your brain to harness a completely conscious mindset that is free from the bondage of self-limiting thinking patterns that will allow you to be totally present to focus on positive emotions that could enhance your compassion and finally understanding yourself and the people around you.

Chapter 14.
Dialectical Behavioral Therapy (DBT)

Dialectical Behavior Therapy, as mentioned earlier, is a form of CBT. The primary difference between the two is that while CBT primarily focuses on change, DBT teaches both acceptance and change. Also, in addition to individual therapy sessions, DBT teaches behavioral skills through group therapy sessions.

DBT was originally developed by Marsha Linehan, PhD, ABPP, in the late 1970s, when she tried to apply standard CBT to women suffering from symptoms of Borderline Personality Disorder, like suicidal tendencies and self-injury. She encountered problems with its use, especially the resistance displayed by patients to the change that is the essence of CBT, and the insufficiency of time to help patients learn the skills they need. Hence, the development of DBT.

The main goal of DBT is to "build a life worth living," which can mean different things to different people. It can mean a successful career for some; a peaceful family life, or a satisfying hobby for others. It is designed to help you.

Essential to DBT is the balancing of two opposing forces: acceptance and change. It is the acceptance of your situation ("you're doing the best you can"), but also recognizing that you need to change, including your behaviors: to be motivated, to grow, and to work harder so that you can reach your goals. (This is where the word "dialectical" in DBT comes in, which describes our way of understanding concepts by considering their opposites.)

And so, who can be helped by Dialectical Behavior Therapy? The common denominator in the problems being treated by DBT is the great need for emotion regulation. This means that people with borderline personality disorder, which exhibit poor control of their emotions in relationships, can benefit from this therapy. In fact, DBT is presently the gold standard in treatments for people with borderline personality disorder. Some of the other problems that DBT can help with include suicidal and self-injuring behaviors, substance abuse, and post-traumatic stress disorder.

How DBT Works

To build a life worth living, which is the main goal of DBT, client and therapist first sit down and make plans. They set their goals and expectations.

There are five components in a standard DBT treatment program: a) skills group, b) individual therapy, c) skills coaching, d) case management, and e) consultation team. This section will just provide an overview on the standard program. A detailed discussion could be found in Chapter 15.

Led by a therapist group leader, group sessions for teaching and learning behavioral skills happen every week and last about 2.5 hours. It is run like a class, and homework assignments are given, so that patients can practice their newfound skills.

Twenty four weeks are required for the entire skills curriculum, and this can be repeated for a 1-year program. Depending on the situation and the needs of the patients, a shorter subset of this curriculum can also be taught.

The Four Skills Modules in DBT
The purpose of this skills group training is to improve clients' capabilities, so that they can effectively deal with the problems and challenges that will arise in their daily lives. They learn from these four skills modules:

1. Mindfulness (being aware of ourselves and the situation we're in),
2. Distress tolerance (learning how to tolerate our pains in tough situations),

3. Interpersonal effectiveness (learning both assertiveness and respect of other people), and
4. Emotion regulation (learning how to change our negative emotions).

Of these four skills modules, mindfulness and distress tolerance belong to the acceptance strategy of DBT; interpersonal effectiveness and emotion regulation belong to the change strategy.

Individual therapy
The purpose of an individual psychotherapy session is to improve the motivation of each patient. Personal issues and struggles are talked about, with the therapist encouraging the patient in the light of DBT's acceptance and change. Skills learned in group sessions are also reinforced. Furthermore, a real relationship of mutual help between therapist and patient is formed; the therapist does become a true partner in the process, not just a teacher or an observer.

Like with the skills group training, individual therapy session also happens every week and runs concurrently with it.

Skills coaching
DBT patients can call their therapists anytime of the day, to ask for advice whenever problems arise. The goal of skills coaching is to train patients to practice and apply in their lives the skills they are learning.

Case management
This is about helping patients manage their own lives. The therapist advises on the things to be done, but intervenes only when necessary.

Consultation team
The therapists themselves are a part of a consultation team, where they are given support for the work they are doing. This way they will stay motivated

and competent. This kind of emotional support is especially needed for difficult cases.

Clients who choose to get Dialectical Behavior Therapy often have several behavioral problems to be treated, not just one. The therapist then will have to prioritize the problems according to the following hierarchy: (1) threatening to life, (2) interference to therapy, (3) interference to quality of life, and (4) the need to learn new skills. For example, suicidal thoughts of a patient will be dealt with first before alcohol abuse.

Lastly, there are 3 to 4 stages of treatment for DBT. Stage 1 corresponds to the initial life of the patient being out-of-control. Stage 2 corresponds to a continued silent suffering after some control has already been achieved. Stage 3 corresponds now to the challenge of living a life: setting goals, gaining self-respect, finding happiness. And Stage 4, which is needed only by some people, corresponds to finding a deeper fulfillment and completeness through spirituality of some kind.

Is Dialectical Behavior Therapy really effective?

So does it really work? The answer is a resounding yes. DBT is a treatment based on pieces of evidences, and research has shown that it is indeed effective against the mental health illnesses it is used on, which are many. It is also found to be effective on people of diverse backgrounds (in terms of age, gender, sexual orientation, and race), and it's already been implemented in more than 25 countries.

DBT has also received recognition from authorities, like the American Psychological Association.

Chapter 15.
Emotional Dysregulation

Emotional dysregulation is, simply put, the incapability of a person to control his or her emotions (and the resulting behaviors) when exposed to situations that trigger those emotions. These situations can be both internal (e.g., thoughts of anger) and external (e.g., harsh criticisms).

Overreacting is another way of putting it. Emotional dysregulation is characterized by an exaggerated display of frustration over something that is probably, to most people, only mildly disappointing. Fits of rage. Weeping. Accusations. Even passive-aggressive behaviors. These are examples of reactions rooted in uncontrolled feelings.

Psychological Disorders Where The Patient Experiences Emotional Dysregulation

Unfortunately, many people often misunderstand individuals suffering from this condition. Because the truth is, it is a condition, a mental health condition to be precise. Emotional dysregulation is often connected to or a part of psychological disorders.

The following is a list of some psychological illnesses where out-of-bounds and out-of-control emotions are a major characteristic:

Borderline Personality Disorder

The essence of this illness is emotional dysregulation itself, in the context of relationships — resulting in unstable relations with other people, and even impulsive and reckless behaviors.

BPD is considered as a serious mental health problem, because some people who have this condition because some people can't manage their emotions properly. Even though some people who have BPD are still highly productive in their workplaces, their private lives could be suffering. They usually suffer from controlling their emotions and thoughts and are often impulsive.

Other mental health concerns such as substance abuse, eating disorders, anxiety disorders, and depression can usually exist alongside BPD. It is not easy to diagnose BPD, and unfortunately, misdiagnosis can affect the person's recovery. Misdiagnosis also happens mainly because of the instability of the patient's mood.

There are crucial differences between these conditions but they all involve mood instability. For those who are suffering from bipolar disorder, the mood swings may happen for several weeks or even months. The mood swings in people who have BPD are noted to be shorter and may just happen within a day.

BPD was only officially recognized as a mental health condition in the 1980s, and so the research is fairly behind compared to other mental disorders. It has also met with massive misconception and public stigma, but cognitive behavior treatments including CBT and DBT have shown to be effective in managing this condition.

Post-Traumatic Stress Disorder

PTSD begins when someone experiences or witnesses a terrifying and traumatic event, and that person has great difficulty in coping and adjusting to the situation for a long time. Flashbacks, nightmares, and anxiety are some of the symptoms of this illness.

Most people who have to go through horrifying events might find it difficult to cope with and adjust to their new situation. But with proper care and suitable CBT or DBT treatment, they usually get better.

The symptoms of PTSD may start to appear within a few weeks of a traumatic event. However, there are also instances that the symptoms appear after several years. PTSD requires intervention if the symptoms are causing major problems in your life such as social, career, or relationships. Most PTSD symptoms can also affect your capacity to perform your everyday routine.

PTSD symptoms are basically categorized into four types: changes in physical and emotional reactions, negative changes in mood and thinking patterns, avoidance, and intrusive memories.

Bipolar Disorder

Once called manic depression, bipolar disorder induces extreme and sudden changes of mood, including emotional highs (mania) and lows (depression). This illness is episodic, happening rarely or many times a year, and can highly and negatively affect a person's life.

Some people who feel heavy depression have the tendency to feel hopeless or sad, and they may even lose their interest in participating in social activities. If the person's moods shift to hypomania or mania, the common result is that the person is either energetic or highly irritable. These sudden shifts in mood could affect your behavior, ability to think clearly, and judgment, and even disrupt resting period.

Mood swings may happen a few times a year or in extreme cases a few times a day. Even though some people may experience some emotional symptoms between episodes, some may never experience anything at all.

Even though bipolar disorder is considered as a lifelong mental health condition, the mood swings and other symptoms could be managed by following a prescribed treatment plan such as medication, CBT or DBT.

Major Depressive Disorder

Also called clinical depression, this illness adversely affects how a person thinks, feels, and behaves by inducing prolonged feelings of sadness and disinterest. Much more than feeling unhappy for some reasons, this kind of depression requires treatment, either by medication or therapy, or both.

The specific cause of MDD is still not fully known, but there are specific factors that are shown to increase the risk of experiencing this condition. Some studies reveal that stress and genes can affect the chemical composition of the brain that reduces its capacity to sustain mood. Hormonal imbalance is also being considered in the development of this mental health disorder.

MDD can also be caused by specific forms of medications that include steroids, specific medical conditions such as hypothyroidism or cancer, and finally drug or alcohol abuse.

Panic Disorder

A person with panic disorder experiences sudden panic attacks, and is very fearful of recurrent attacks. Symptoms include palpitations, sweating, trembling, chest pains, and nausea. This illness, like the others, severely limits what he or she can do and accomplish.

Around 6 million adults in the US are suffering from panic disorder. Women are also more prone to the condition compared to men. The condition may usually start in early adulthood or late adolescence. Take note that not all people who experience panic episodes develop panic disorder. Some only experience isolated, single attack.

For a formal diagnosis of panic disorder, a person should experience persistent worry or concern about a panic attack or the result of having one such as going insane or even death. Also, the person should also demonstrate avoidance behaviors that are related to perceived triggers of the attack such as unfamiliar places or exercise.

Obsessive-Compulsive Disorder

People with OCD are disturbed by recurring and unwelcome thoughts and sensations (obsessions), and are compelled to do some things repetitively against their will, like washing of hands, arranging and ordering things, and counting. This condition is obviously distressing to the people who have it, as they are being prevented from having a full life.

It is just normal for most of us to have repetitive behaviors or focused thoughts. However, these don't intervene in our daily lives and may even make our daily tasks easier. For individuals who have OCD, the thoughts are persistent, and unwanted behaviors and routines should be followed, and not doing them may cause significant stress.

Some people who have OCD believe that their obsessions are not true, while others believe that their obsessions might be true. Despite their awareness, most people who have OCD find it hard to veer away from their obsessions or stopping compulsive actions.

To be formally diagnosed, those who suspect they have OCD must have obsession as well as compulsion that could be time-consuming, result in major distress, and interferes social life, work, and other significant aspects in their lives.

Narcissistic Personality Disorder

People with narcissistic personality suffer from excessive love of oneself and of one's own importance, and they have a deep need for admiration and attention. Behind this facade of confidence, however, is a brittle self-esteem that is easily bruised. All these result in troubled relationships, disappointments, and a lack of empathy for others.

People who have NPD believe they are special or superior, and usually try to affiliate with other people whom they think are also special or superior in different ways. This affiliation improves their self-confidence that is often quite weak beneath the surface.

Those who have NPD often seek too much admiration, praise, or attention. They need to know if other people are thinking highly of them. They also have difficulty in tolerating defeat or criticism, and could be left empty or humiliated if they experience damage from rejection or criticism.

Histrionic Personality Disorder

A persistent pattern of attention-seeking and an overmuch display of emotions mark the people with histrionic personality. Often lively and dramatic, even sexually provocative, they nevertheless become easily depressed when they are not the center of attention. They also exhibit manipulative and codependency behaviors. Needless to say, their relationships are beset with problems.

People who have this disorder demonstrate too much emotion, and they have the tendency to be emotional in most settings. They are also considered as seeking too much attention.

Those who have this disorder feel unappreciated and uncomfortable if they think they are not in the limelight. The resulting behavior may include striking self-centeredness, theatricality, self-dramatization, seeking approval or attention, and even sexual seductiveness even in situations that are considered inappropriate.

Most people who have this disorder could be seen as lively or dramatic and may even charm strangers with their openness, enthusiasm, and even flirtatiousness. However, they could also embarrass people around them with too much emotion like crying uncontrollably over minor things, embracing casual acquaintances, and temper tantrums.

These psychological disorders clearly show that dysregulated emotions have varied causes that are rooted in mental health issues. Still, people with traumatic injuries to the brain can also manifest emotions that are out of control, along with other debilitating conditions associated with brain problems. Such injuries can be caused by physical shock, stroke, cancer, infection, drugs and alcohol, and diseases affecting the neurons of the brain.

Emotional dysregulation then, in other words, is not simply a matter of character flaw. People may judge you and misunderstand you because of it, but you don't have to endure the persecution and the self-blame. It is a serious medical condition, and it is probably only a small part of a bigger psychological problem. And so, if you suspect that you are suffering from it, then what you need to do is get help.

Emotional Dysregulation and DBT

Having looked at some of the psychological disorders associated with emotional dysregulation, we can only conclude that any treatment to be used on people suffering from these illnesses must be something pretty special — something that is designed to take into account the exceptionally high levels and exceptionally high amounts of emotions involved in the process.

Dialectical Behavior Therapy is exactly that -- specialized. It is first and foremost designed to treat psychological disorders involving dysregulated emotions, like borderline personality disorder. As mentioned above, DBT is the gold standard treatment for people with BPD.

Two characteristics of DBT stand out as the reasons why it is especially suited as an effective treatment to emotional dysregulation. The first one is its dialectical nature, the careful balancing of change and acceptance. The second one is its highly structured and highly systematic approach to treatment.

When DBT was first being developed by Dr. Linehan and her team, using standard Cognitive Behavioral Therapy on patients suffering from symptoms of borderline personality disorder adult women with histories of suicidal ideation, chronic suicide attempts, urges to do self-harm, and self-mutilation" — one of the problems they encountered was the high degree of resistance displayed by patients to change. Change is the essence of CBT, and while this works for some people, it became apparent to them that it doesn't work quite well on its own in intensely emotional situations.

When someone is hurting deeply and is contemplating ending his life, the last thing he needs is for his therapist to tell him that he must change. Instead, what he needs most — at this point in his life — is understanding and acceptance. Validation this is called, the recognition that his opinions and feelings are important, and that they make sense in some way. But of course, he still needs to change, especially his destructive tendencies, so that his life can become worth living.

Balancing change with acceptance, then, is one key reason why DBT is quite effective in dealing with emotional dysregulation.

The other key reason, DBT's structured and systematic approach to treatment, is also quite useful in countering the negative aspects of emotions-intensive therapy.

Unlike other forms of therapy which flow freely and are introspective, this structured and systematic approach to treatment prevents undue stress on the already bruised and fragile emotions of the patients. In group therapy sessions, for example, patients are being taught, in school-fashion, the skills they need so that they can live better. The orderly atmosphere of this setting makes sure that the patients are as emotionally comfortable as possible while they learn these skills.

In the next section, we will look into core DBT skills. As a review, there are four skills modules in DBT: mindfulness, distress tolerance, interpersonal effectiveness, and emotion regulation.

Chapter 16.
Core DBT Skills

Each one of us, at one time or another, had some cause for regret when we had let our emotions dictate our actions — to our consternation and shame. Perhaps someone had criticized us unfairly and severely, and we could not help answering back with harsh words. Sometimes we are given the chance to take back the things we've said, or to ask for forgiveness for the things we've done. But there are times when the damage we inflicted is too much that trust could no longer be rebuilt, and so, we have no choice but to deal with the consequences -- a broken relationship perhaps, or a lost opportunity at work.

Can you imagine then what it's like for people who are constantly struggling, and failing, to control their negative emotions? Their anger? Depression? Frustration? Hopelessness? If we already feel ashamed of our occasional mistakes, how much more are their shame? And how much more devastating are the consequences of their inability for good emotional control?

The main goal of Dialectical Behavior Therapy is to build a life worth living, and the purpose of a DBT skills group is to improve people's capabilities to deal with the challenges and problems in their lives by teaching them behavioral skills, especially in regards to their thoughts and emotions.

As mentioned, a DBT skills group is a weekly group therapy session, headed by a therapist, lasts for about 2 1/2 hours, and is run like a school class. This is in addition to the weekly individual therapy session for each patient.

There are four categories, or modules, of these DBT skills.

The first one is **Mindfulness,** and it is about learning to become aware of ourselves and our situation at this moment — what we are thinking right now, what we are feeling (physically or emotionally), what we are seeing, hearing, smelling, etc.

The second one is called **Distress Tolerance,** and it is about accepting and tolerating our pains and the circumstances we're in, and not change them, especially when things get more difficult.

The third one is called **Interpersonal Effectiveness,** and it is about learning self-respect, assertiveness (e.g., asking for what we need, or saying no), and respect of and interaction with other people, especially in tough situations.

The fourth one is called **Emotion Regulation,** and it is about understanding and containing our emotions, and about behaving appropriately in response to those emotions.

The one thing to remember is that, with these DBT skills, there is certainly hope for better control of ourselves — our thoughts, our emotions, our behaviors. Therefore, there is also hope for a better kind of life than what we have now.

Mindfulness is also a core skill for CBT and ACT so it's crucial that you master it. It has been discussed in a previous chapter, along with the exercises you could try in order to boost mindfulness. So now, we will discuss the rest.

Distress Tolerance

Distress tolerance is learning "how to tolerate pain in difficult situations, not change it." The question now that may be in your mind is, why tolerate pain at all? Why not avoid it?

Unlike most approaches to mental health treatment, which concentrate on changing the situations that cause pain, Dialectical Behavior Therapy teaches tolerance and acceptance of pain and distress. After all, these are part of life and cannot be fully avoided. Such tolerance is also part of growing up. Denial of pain and distress — running away from them — only increases our suffering, and impedes our growth and progress.

Going back to our example, suppose again that your boss has not been impressed by the self-control you've displayed when he criticized you, and his behavior has degenerated into outright verbal abuse. He has even threatened to fire you. You know then that something is very wrong, and that you need to do something, but your emotions are already starting to overwhelm you. You are seeing red, with your anger much greater than before, and all you want to do now is curse your boss. Maybe even hit him. You are in a crisis situation which could cost you your job.

DBT's distress tolerance skills can help you survive circumstances like this, and more. You could not have avoided the situation; it is beyond your control. But by applying these skills you can put up with it and not make the situation worse.

There are two groups of these skills for distress tolerance. The first group, which applies to our example, is called Crisis Survival Skills, and they are to help us endure painful and sudden events, impulses, and emotions when there is still nothing we can do about them. The second group is called Reality Acceptance Skills, and they are to help us accept and live our lives fully, even if our lives are not ideal for us, so that our suffering will lessen.

Crisis Survival Skills

Crisis Survival Skills, as the name suggests, are to be used in crisis situations, and only in these situations. As their purpose is only to help us endure such crises, they are not to be used for everyday problems.

You are in a crisis if you find yourself in an extremely stressful situation, where heavy demands are being made upon you, and where you need to make some kind of decision right away. You can use these survival skills then, especially if you are in great pain and are in danger of being overpowered by your emotions.

There are six of these skills, and they are (1) The STOP Skill, (2) Pros and Cons, (3) Changing Body Chemistry (TIP), (4) Distracting (ACCEPTS), (5) Self-Soothing, and (6) Improving the Moment (IMPROVE).

Mnemonics are utilized in order to help you retain the information so you can have it ready when you need it the most.

The STOP Skill
This skill can prevent us from acting impulsively on our emotions, which can make an already difficult situation even worse. In such settings where you are highly tempted to yield to your emotion mind, simply STOP yourself:

1. **Stop.** Freeze. Just don't move. Don't do anything rash.
2. **Take a step back.** Take yourself away from what is happening — emotionally, mentally, physically.
3. **Observe** the real situation, take note of other people, and take note of yourself.
4. **Proceed** mindfully, acting with awareness and considering what is best for the situation, other people, and yourself.

Pros and Cons Technique
Pros and Cons can be used when we need to decide between two actions: acting on the crisis impulses, or resisting them. Of course, our real goal is to resist (tolerate) these impulses or urges, because giving in to them is destructive in the long run.

Make a list of pros and cons for acting on those impulses. Then make another list of pros and cons for resisting then.

And then, while you are still not in a crisis, study them, memorize them, take them to heart, so that when a crisis does come, you are ready.

Changing Body Chemistry (TIP)
This skill is used to quickly decrease the intensity of our raging emotion mind. Whenever you find yourself nearly losing control, simply TIP the odds in your favor:

Bring down the *temperature* of your face by dunking it in a bowl of cold water, holding your breath for 30 seconds. Or place a bag of cold water on your eyes and cheeks.

You can also burn your energy by doing some *Intense* exercises.

Or you can perform *Paced breathing* — inhaling deeply and exhaling slowly, until the rate of your breathing slows down.

Or you can try Paired muscle relaxation — tensing your body while breathing in deeply, and then relaxing it as you exhale.

Distractions (ACCEPTS Technique)
Distraction is another useful way to help us survive crises. It reduces our exposure to whatever it is that brings us distress. And so, whenever you find yourself in an emotional bind, simply let go of your pride and remember that a wise person ACCEPTS help and knows the value of distraction by:

Get **Active**
Engage in any activity. Clean your room. Watch a movie. Walk your dog. Eat.

Contribute *to a cause you're passionate about, or to the happiness of somebody you love.*

Instead of ranting about the unfairness of it all, call your mother and tell her how much you love her.

Compare
Perform a comparison of the here-and-now and the better times. Compare your own miserable life with the lives of those who are more miserable than you. Just this one time, let yourself get some perspective by thinking about people who have it worse that you do – you can even engage in a little schadenfreude.

*Explore different **emotions***
Get all weepy watching a soap opera. Read romance novels and get excited. Or watch the funniest movies you can find. And just laugh.

Push *away the entire situation for a while*
Pretend it doesn't exist. If there is just one time where denial is allowed, this is it.

*Allow other **thoughts** to occupy your mind*
Do anything that will rivet your attention, if only for a short time. Answer crossword puzzles. Solve math problems. Write a computer program.

*Feel other **sensations**.*
Allow yourself to feel sharp sensations. Take a hot shower. Listen to rock music. Turn the fan/AC to the max.

Self-Soothing
Self-soothing means indulging ourselves, especially our five senses, to relieve our pains and distress.

When you need to self-soothe, simply do things that are pleasurable to your senses, like smelling flowers, listening to soft instrumental music, or eating your favorite ice cream.

Improving the Moment (IMPROVE)
When in a crisis, the situation may be out of our control, but we can make the difficult moment better for us, on how we experience it. Consequently, this can give us a better handle on our emotions.

To use this technique during the moment of your crisis, and experience an improvement on how you cope, you can do the following:

Fill your mind with **Imagery**. Remember a time in your past when you were very happy, and relive it. Or just imagine a peaceful scene, with you in the center.

Find a deeper **Meaning** to your life, or to the situation.

Find comfort in **Prayer**, if you're the spiritual kind.

Find rest in **Relaxing** activities.

Focus only on **One** thing at the moment, like your breathing, or whatever else you're doing.

Reward yourself with a brief **Vacation**. Or any extended break.

Encourage yourself. Say something affirmative out loud, such as "I can do this!"

Reality Acceptance Skills

There are five Reality Acceptance Skills that can help us accept the unchangeable facts of our lives, and so lead us to a place of less suffering, perhaps even of joy and contentment.

These five skills are (1) Radical Acceptance, (2) Turning the Mind, (3) Willingness, (4) Half-smiling and Willing Hands, and (5) Allowing the Mind.

Radical Acceptance
Our lives are not perfect; we are not perfect. There are always some things that we want to change for the better: in our job, in our family, in our relationships, in our body, in our character. And we all make mistakes — sometimes terrible mistakes — mistakes that may have placed us in this distressing condition we're in right now.

Radical Acceptance is about being totally open and without resistance to these facts of our lives. We accept our situations, our past and our present. We accept our mistakes and the consequences of those mistakes. We accept that there are things we just can't change. We accept that there is a limit to what the future can hold for us. And we accept who and what we are.

Accepting reality, however, doesn't mean that we approve of it, or that we don't want to change some aspects of it. But reality does need to be accepted, even if it is painful, because rejecting it doesn't change it — denial only leads to more suffering. On the other hand, acceptance does bring peace, and eventually, it does lead to some change.

Turning the Mind
Turning the Mind is the first step to accepting reality. It is choosing to put ourselves, despite the many issues that hinder us, into the path of acceptance.

But acceptance is not a one-time event, but a journey where there are many opportunities for turning back. And so turning the mind is actually choosing to accept reality again and again... and again.

Willingness (and allowing it to manifest physically)
Willingness is simply the eagerness to live life fully. It means doing what is needed in each situation, mindfully and wisely. It means giving it our best.

These are two ways where we can show our acceptance of reality with our body. A Half-smile is exactly that, a half-smile with a peaceful facial expression.

Willing Hands, on the other hand, is keeping our arms relaxed, with our hands open and turned outward, as if showing our willingness to receive whatever it is that life brings.

Allowing the Mind
Allowing the Mind is simply the mindful observation of our thoughts, with the apparent purpose of helping us accept and love who we are.

To conclude this section, we have now learned what distress tolerance is, its benefits, and the two groups of skills associated with it: crisis survival, and reality acceptance. For sure, learning these skills, even if we're not undergoing DBT, will empower us immensely in our daily lives.

There is something very beautiful in people who are able to handle themselves well in crises, and also those who exude peace and contentment, after having fully accepted their lot in life.

Interpersonal Effectiveness

Interpersonal Effectiveness is all about building and maintaining relationships, and dealing with conflicts. It is also concerned about having a healthy outlook of one's self in the context of relationships.

Building a life worth living is the main goal of Dialectical Behavior Therapy, and having effective interpersonal skills, needless to say, is a requirement for such a life. "No man is an island," says the old proverb. As people, we need each other, and much of what give our lives meaning (or pain) are based on the kind of relationships that we have, or don't have.

Unfortunately, we only need to take a look at the heartbreaking statistics of broken and dysfunctional families to realize that many people just don't know how, or don't have what it takes to make their relationships work.

The reasons and causes why relationships fail are varied and as numerous. We can, however, look at this situation in a simplified manner, and identify several factors that bar the way to effective interpersonal relations.

These factors are (1) lack of interpersonal skills, (2) unclear and unbalanced objectives in the relationship, (3) uncontrolled emotions, (4) not enough consideration of the future, (5) other people standing in the way, and (6) one's thoughts and beliefs.

As one of DBT's four skills modules, Interpersonal Effectiveness fits into the larger purpose of improving people's capabilities by teaching them behavioral skills, so that they can successfully and effectively deal with the problems and challenges of their lives. Interpersonal Effectiveness, as practiced in DBT, has three main goals: (1) to learn how to get what you want and need from other people, (2) to learn how to build (and end) relationships, and (3) to learn how to balance relationships, also called walking the middle path.

We will discuss the skills that are centered on the first and second of these goals. The third goal, walking the middle path, already deals with the complex and internal issues of a relationship, and so we will no longer discuss it.

These skills teach us how to get what we want from other people (objectives effectiveness), while also preserving the relationship (relationship effectiveness) and our self-respect (self-respect effectiveness).

Objectives Effectiveness (DEAR MAN)

There are some valid reasons why we can insist on the things we want in a relationship, such as getting our basic human rights (especially in the case of abuse), and saying no to unreasonable demands. We can also insist on our way when there is some conflict we want to solve, or when we simply want our opinions to be heard.

When there is something you want from that someone you love, just follow this DEAR MAN strategy:

If the reason is unclear as to why you are demanding, **Describe** it. Tell it unambiguously with facts.

Then **Express** what you feel and think about the matter. Don't assume that these are already obvious.

Next, **Assert** yourself. Ask clearly what you want from your beloved. Or say no emphatically.

Next, **Reinforce** the positive consequences if your desire is granted (or if needed, the negative consequences if it is not granted). Don't forget to reward your man (or woman) if the first happened.

If those techniques don't work, then bring it up to the next level.

Stay **Mindful**. Don't give up, and don't get distracted. Just keep expressing and asserting yourself, even if you're already under attack.

Be sure also to *Appear* confident. Don't show any sign of diffidence and wavering.

But be willing also to *Negotiate*, to compromise if needed, or to ask for something else.

Relationship Effectiveness (GIVE)

When we make our demands, we must also be careful that we don't put our relationship at risk. And so when you ask for something, you must also GIVE something:

Be *Gentle* with your beloved. Don't harass. Don't scorn. Don't judge. And don't make any threats if you are not getting what you want.

Act *Interested*. Listen. Make eye contact. Consider the other person's point of view.

Then *Validate* with your words and your actions. Show him or her that you understand, that you really are listening, and that what he or she is saying is important to you.

Lastly, use an *Easy* manner. Smile. Be wonderful to the one you love.

Self-respect Effectiveness (FAST)

When we make demands, we must also be careful that we don't put our self-respect at risk. Hold FAST to the following principles to safeguard yourself:

Be *Fair* to yourself and to your beloved. Make sure that both of you feel important and valued, regardless of your difference of opinion.

Make no *Apologies* when there is nothing to be sorry for. You have the right to disagree, and the right to ask for what you need.

Stick to your *values*. Defend your integrity. You don't have to compromise if it runs counter to your morality.

Lastly, be *Truthful*. Don't lie or pretend just to get what you want.

Building and Ending Relationships

Finding and Getting People to Like You

Relationships require hard work, and this is already true when we are only just starting to look for friends. The following are some advice on how to find those people we can call our friends, and with whom we can share our lives with.

Look for people who are already familiar with you, say your coworkers. Familiarity can lead to friendship, and sometimes love.

Look for people who share your values, principles, and interests. Friendships are often formed among people who have similar passions.

Work hard to improve your conversational skills.

Take some risks in letting people know that you like them. They might like you back.

Finally, make some effort to join a group conversation, especially if it looks like the group is open to new members.

Mindfulness of Others

Our relationships last longer if we are mindful of them – and the people in our lives. To this end, we use the "what" skills of mindfulness (observe, describe, participate) in our interactions with people.

For example, suppose you are spending some time with a lady friend. You give her your full attention during this time, and you make sure that distractions, like you answering a phone call, are kept to a minimum (this is observation).

When the two of you chat, you mostly talk about what happened to both of your lives, avoiding any unfounded assumptions or gossips (this is description).

Finally, you simply enjoy the time you have with her, laughing and having fun (this is participation).

Ending Destructive Relationships
Sometimes you are confronted with the choice of ending a relationship, either because it is abusive or your personal welfare is in danger, or because it prevents you from pursuing your goals and from enjoying the other aspects of life.

Whatever the reason, the decision to end it and your subsequent actions should be done with your wise mind, not emotion mind.

You must also plan ahead and ready yourself emotionally for the coming breakup.

Then carry out your decision. Use the DEAR MAN, GIVE, and FAST interpersonal skills you've just learned.

Most important of all, if the relationship is really abusive and your life may be in danger if you try to break it off, ask first for help and support from authorities.

To conclude this section, we have now learned what interpersonal effectiveness is, its importance, and some of the skills associated with it. As humans, we are made for relationships, and it is to our great well-being if the relationships that we have in this life are as problem-free as possible. We may not avail of DBT ourselves, but learning these interpersonal effectiveness skills are sure to help us in many and wonderful ways.

CHAPTER 17.
EMOTION REGULATION

In our discussion of mindfulness skills, we've already talked about controlling our emotional responses by balancing our reasonable mind and our emotion mind — which results in our use of the Wise Mind, where we recognize both our reason and emotions, and then act accordingly.

In our discussion of distress tolerance skills, we've also talked about emotional control, first in crisis situations, and then in accepting the reality of our lives.

And now in our discussion of emotion regulation, we will dig a bit deeper into these matters. We will study emotions themselves, learn how to change them, and how to be less vulnerable to them.

Complete control of our emotions is impossible. After all, we are still humans, and feelings are an integral part of us. However, it is possible to have an increasing measure of control over them, so that we do not become (or cease to become) their slaves. This kind of mastery gives us a sense of freedom, and a sense of hope too, that perhaps we are indeed the true masters of our fate.

Dialectical Behavior Therapy is specially designed for people suffering from emotional dysregulation, and studies have shown that it is indeed an effective treatment. We've already covered some DBT skills that help us better manage our emotions and our responses to it, but now we will look further into this particular aspect of DBT: emotion regulation skills.

Emotion Regulation has the following goals: (1) to understand our own emotions and to give them names, (2) to lower the occurrence of emotions we don't want, (3) to lower our vulnerability to Emotion Mind, and (4) to reduce our suffering when painful emotions do overcome us.

Emotion regulation skills typically involve understanding emotions, changing emotional responses and reducing one's vulnerability to the emotion mind.

Understanding and Identifying Emotions

Emotions are an important part of us as human beings. What would we be, and what would our lives be like, if we are without emotions?

Admittedly, emotions do become a problem — or the cause of a multitude of problems — especially if they run amok. Still, they are important, and they have roles to play in our lives.

For example, our emotions can motivate us, and they can be the driving force behind our success, helping us overcome obstacles after obstacles. Emotions, when harnessed properly, can also become great tools for communication. An impassioned speech is more likely to trigger action than a dry talk. Furthermore, our emotions, with proper discernment, can tell us something about our situation or our environment, like when there is some danger that we cannot see.

Our subject here, however, is regulating our emotions, so that our feelings, especially the negative ones, do not get out of hand. And there are indeed some factors that do prevent effective control of our emotions, such as biological factors, lack of skills, emotional overload, and erroneous beliefs. DBT deals with some of these factors.

Emotions are a complex process, and we probably don't need to know how exactly they happen. What is important for us is to be able to identify their different kinds, because that is the first step towards gaining control. Knowledge is power, as they say.

Do you feel angry, disgusted, or envious? Are you fearful, jealous, or happy? Do you feel shame, or do you feel love? And why do you think you feel this way?

Changing Emotional Responses

Sometimes, we find the resolve to change our emotional response to a situation, simply because we do not want what we are feeling. It can be anger, shame, guilt, or despair.

The following skills can help you do just that: change your emotions.

Fact checking

This simply means that we should ascertain whether our thoughts, feelings, or behaviors agree, or are reasonable responses to the events that cause them. This is because our own interpretations of events can be wrong, and this in turn can cause us to make erroneous responses.

Opposite Action

Opposite action means doing just the opposite of what our present emotion is inciting us to do, which is also called the "action urge" of that particular emotion. For example, if you are feeling angry with someone, your tendency is to attack that person. The opposite action of this is to gently try to avoid the confrontation.

Opposite action, however, is not always the best thing to do, but there are two situations where this is advisable. The first one is when, after checking the facts, you found out that your emotion is an unreasonable response to what has caused it. The second one is when acting on your emotion will not result in anything good, and will probably only worsen the situation. It doesn't matter then if your emotion is justified or not.

Problem Solving

When the emotion you want to change is reasonable or is justified, then what you can do is to either avoid the situation or try to change it — so that your emotion can change too.

Problem solving is to try to change the situation that causes your unwanted emotion. It begins by you identifying the problem by considering all the facts.

Next, you set your goal (one that will make you feel alright), and then you brainstorm and ask advice for possible solutions.

Finally, you try out each promising solution until the problem is solved.

Reducing Vulnerability to Emotion Mind

The good news is that, with time and with practice, our resilience to emotional disturbances and our resistance to emotion mind can be built up.

The following skills can help you strengthen your heart, so to speak:

Accumulate Positive Emotions

This is like continually depositing money in the bank, so that when a time of great financial need comes, you have savings to withdraw money from. But instead of money and instead of a real bank, you deposit good emotions and happy experiences in your heart and mind. And so, when a time of crisis, tragedy, or any other difficulty comes, you will have this reservoir of positive energy and positive memories to draw strength from.

Accumulating positive emotions has both short-term and long-term goals. In a short-term goal, you do now what you can to experience pleasant things. In a long-term goal, you make some changes in your life so that more good things will happen to you in the future. Extending our analogy, you not only deposit money today, but you also make some investments, so that someday your income will exponentially increase.

Build Mastery and Cope Ahead

Building mastery is doing things that will give you a sense of accomplishment and competence. This can be a new hobby that teaches you skills you don't know before — or anything that stretches you and makes you grow. The confidence that you gain from this will become part of your preparedness to deal with difficult situations.

Coping ahead, on the other hand, is planning and training to deal with the emotional battles when they come. This includes analysis of possible problems, consideration of possible solutions, and even rehearsing in your own mind your possible responses.

Taking Care of Your Mind by Taking Care of Your Body

A healthy body means a healthy resistance to negative emotions. Keep your body healthy by making sure that you seek treatment for physical illness, eat a balanced diet, avoid mood-altering substances, sleep adequately, and exercise.

To conclude this section, we have now learned what emotions are, and what emotion regulation is. We've also learned its importance, and some of the skills associated with it. Keep in mind that there are ways where we can become masters of our own emotions — to never again feel helpless and at the mercy of our own feelings.

CHAPTER 18.
ACCEPTANCE AND COMMITMENT THERAPY (ACT)

It is natural for humans to suffer. However, suffering is not just about physical or psychological pain. People also suffer from difficult self-assessments, uncomfortable feelings, and painful memories. Because we dread or worry about suffering, we do everything to avoid them. We want to minimize our suffering. Many of us give importance to feeling better. But a good life is a lot more than just the absence of suffering. We want to live a good life and we want to make the best of our short stay on this planet.

Acceptance and Commitment Therapy (ACT) is focused on the problem of human suffering, but also beyond that. It is also about understanding human suffering as an important factor in realizing a good life. This new form of CBT is focused on important questions such as "What is my real purpose in life?"

But before we delve deeper into ACT as a specific CBT technique, let us first understand human suffering

Understanding Human Suffering in the Context of Psychotherapy

For pets, perhaps a cat or a dog, happiness is pretty much easier to achieve. If their basic needs are provided - food, water, shelter, warmth, and fun - they will be happy. With the absence of human intervention, pets usually miss some of these fundamental needs. They live their lives as mere animals. In comparison, humans may also miss fundamental needs, too. It can be easy to understand how miserable a person can get when these needs aren't met.

However, many of us have all the things that some people are happy to have, but we are still not happy. With our modern wonders - technology, supermarkets, real estate - we are entertained, well fed, and protected from cold or heat. But still, many of us are still miserable.

We still hear stories about billionaires on their prime committing suicide. There are celebrities who have already achieved wealth and fame but still sulk in the corner then drink alcohol or take drugs. It seems that our lives naturally come with suffering.

Physical pain has distinct psychological (mind) and physiological (body) components that manifest response and stimulus. The biological aspect of pain refers to the signal that is transmitted to our brain so we are aware that something is wrong.

On the other hand, the psychological aspect of pain dwells on the meaning or interpretation we provide to that message - our self-dialogue that involves our personal beliefs which then trigger our emotional responses. Human suffering results from emotional and mental responses to pain. The psychological and biological facets of chronic pain work together to function like radar that helps us keep track of our psychological wellbeing.

The resolve to recover from chronic pain is distinct between the actual pain and suffering. It is also then focused on achieving comfort. While we cannot avoid pain, we can surely do something about our response to suffering, pretty much like how we can respond to anger.

In the psychological context, pain is a function that alerts us about the imbalance in our physical, mental, and spiritual aspect. Anything that affects the body or mind could also affect the other self-dimensions. Recovery from human suffering can be progressive, gradual, or a continuous process of restoring balance in these dimensions.

Human suffering is regarded as both a cause and effect of distressing emotions and catastrophic thoughts associated with pain. This may include helplessness, hopelessness, loneliness, shame, guilt, frustration, depression, fear, anger, irritability, and anxiety.

The bad habit of negative thinking can also make our situations seem worse than the actual situation. Most people, especially those who are not suffering from chronic pain, tend to magnify the negative aspects of the situation through overthinking. Our minds are capable of making us miserable, and negative thinking could become a self-defeating and self-fulfilling prediction.

For those who are suffering from chronic pain, there is a direct link between the level of pain and negative thinking. It can be a dangerous cycle in which pain could result in negative thinking and self-doubt that translate to emotions that coincide with human suffering. This experience could increase stress and muscle tension that in turn could amplify the pain signals that trigger more pain.

The progression of human suffering can be like this:

- Pain results in negative thinking or self-doubt
- Negative thinking or self-doubt results to negative feelings such as sadness or depression
- Sadness or depression could lead to stress or muscle tension
- Stress or muscle tension could lead to more pain
- Pain results in more negative thinking and self-doubt

As you can see, it's a vicious cycle, and the longer this cycle continues, the more we become out of balance.

We can do something about human suffering when we become more aware of the cycle and learn how we respond differently to our pain. The recovery process for pain includes significantly modifying the negative progression beginning with the cognitive and emotional balance through mindfulness and acceptance strategies.

By restoring balance, you can counteract the dynamics of deviation. Once you become aware of your negative thoughts you can harness yourself to accept the situation and detach from it. This will then lead to a decreased feeling of negative emotions that will result in less muscle tension and stress.

Again, this is not supposed to be easy. But it is completely possible if you work on it. By adjusting our thoughts, and how we think about our thoughts, we can effectively reshape our emotional responses including the extent to which we suffer.

ACT - Experienced Based Psych`otherapy

ACT, expressed as a single word and not phonetic letters, is a new form of CBT that is gaining a lot of attention in recent years. It emphasizes values, acceptance, mindfulness and processes to help people overcome life hurdles.

The concept of human suffering as a natural and unavoidable aspect of humanity is a fundamental assumption of ACT. It also revolves around the attempt of people to take control or avoid their own experiences that could lead to human suffering and other areas that are not working in our lives. ACT can help people learn effective ways of managing pain, practicing mindfulness, obtain clarity on what is really important, and to seek a life with more meaning. The objective of ACT is not to get rid of pain, but instead to learn how to experience life without too much struggle.

ACT is regarded as an empirical psychotherapy because its researchers and practitioners are committed to the progress of science and the empirical assessment of its causes and effects.

As of 2014, ACT has been scrutinized in more than 80 randomized clinical trials for different concerns in studies with more than 5,000 subjects. This form of CBT has also been used to build a non-therapeutic version of the same processes known as Acceptance and Commitment Training, which is focused on the development of values skills, acceptance, and mindfulness.

Relational Frame Theory

The Relational Frame Theory (RFT) frames the fundamental concept of ACT. RFT aims to explore the link between behavior and human language.

Understanding language is crucial in psychotherapy. Many of us use language in private when we think or in public when we speak with the people around us. We use language to think about, read about, write about, talk about, evaluate, relate, categorize, and describe everything around us.

Language is a useful tool in our existence as human beings, and without it we may never had the chance to build our civilizations. For example, without language, we cannot develop laws and societal rules to regulate our behavior.

While human language offers a lot of benefits, it could also have negative aspects. It's like the yin and yang - it has a powerful dark side and the powerful bright side. And based on RFT, language plays a critical role in human suffering. Language is a tool we use to form prejudiced and hateful assumptions about people around us, construct negative thoughts, obsess over things, and revisit events that caused us trauma in the past. Too much use of language and thinking could also make it hard to keep in touch with the present moment. We could spend so much time in thinking about our past and worrying about our future that we end up being unable to enjoy the present.

Through a deeper understanding of human language and its mechanism, we can better harness its bright side to minimize the effects of the dark side. This form of understanding is what RFT is trying to provide through ACT.

Psychotherapists who are studying how human language affects our behavior usually concentrate on two remarkable aspects of language: generativity and symbolism.

It is easy to understand symbolism as language is used to refer to an object or an idea. For example, the word "tree" refers to a type of plant with a trunk that supports branches, leaves, and may or may not bear flowers or fruits. Language is used to symbolize things. When you gain a better understanding of a specific word, then you can understand its meaning.

Meanwhile, generativity refers to our ability to create and understand an endless number of sentences with meaning. It is also known as productivity. Every language has a specific number of basic letters, sounds, and words. However, each one of us can produce an endless number of totally unique sentences with these words, letters, and sounds.

Various theories have been developed to explore these features and usually describe the important properties or concentrate on various concerns. For instance, linguists believe that the novelty and complexity and generativity of language are mainly due to genetic factors. However, cognitive psychologists believe that our brain is responsible for how we process and store information including symbolisms.

In spite of the differences in focus, most language studies are based on the similar idea that language is used to express information that is developed by our brains. Basically, language is a system of symbols that will allow us to express our ideas that can be understood by other people. These theories often concentrate on what are deemed to be the important processes of language.

Researchers and practitioners of RFT take a different method of exploring language and cognition. Instead of explaining language as a means of communicating ideas from one person to another, RFT focuses on how humans obtain language through interaction with people and their environment. This is framed to provide a useful and practical language analysis and cognition and not just a description of a concept.

ACT is considered as the applied technology of RFT as it tries to help people use language as a way to resolve specific psychological issues. This can be done through the psychological flexibility model that is distinct in ACT.

The Psychological Flexibility Model

The main objective in undergoing ACT is to enhance our psychological flexibility, which refers to our capacity to keep in touch with the present as a fully aware human being, and depending on what the circumstances call for, persisting or changing in behavior to serve preferred values.

To put this simply, this means taking our own emotions and thoughts a bit more lightly, and behaving on long-term values instead of momentary feelings and thoughts, and impulses.

This could happen because emotions and thoughts tend to be shaky indicators for long-term values. It's not easy to control them, and they have the tendency to go to extremes. When we always allow our emotions and thoughts to influence our behavior, we might overlook the more significant, emerging trends of action and fail to grasp genuine meaning in our lives, or experience life's richness.

At present, psychological flexibility is measured through the Acceptance and Action Questionnaire, which is used by psychotherapists and ACT specialists to predict the following psychological concerns:

- Depression
- Poor work performance
- Substance abuse
- Anxiety sensitivity
- Long-term disability
- Higher anxiety
- General pathology
- Alexithymia
- Worry

There are six fundamental ACT processes that establish psychological flexibility, and these will be discussed in detail in the next chapter. Take note that each process is considered as a positive psychological skill and not a special technique to resolve psychological concerns.

Chapter 19.
The Six Fundamental ACT Processes

Basically, ACT is focused on the six core processes that revolve around psychological flexibility. This largely defines the expansive way to frame our thoughts. It is important to take note that all these processes work with each other and not as individual techniques for psychotherapy.

The six processes of ACT are acceptance, being present, cognitive defusion, committed action, self as context, and values.

Acceptance

Acceptance is considered as an alternative approach for experiential avoidance. It also involves the conscious and active acceptance of personal history without trying to change its form or frequency, especially if doing so will result in damage to the person's psychological health.

For instance, people who are suffering from anxiety are encouraged to feel anxiety as an emotion that is natural for people to feel. Meanwhile, people who are suffering from chronic pain are encouraged to undergo specific treatments that will allow them to cope. Take note that this process is not an end in itself. Instead, it is developed as a way to increase actions that are based on values.

Most people who are suffering from anxiety usually find it odd when they are advised by their ACT specialists to accept something that has been causing them suffering. This may not make sense initially. Some people ask "Why would we want to accept anxiety? Doesn't that mean that we have to live with this harmful emotion?"

But that's the ACT way. The process requires acceptance, after which you will have to go. It may sound contradictory because how can you let go of something that you have already accepted?

Keep in mind that language is used to represent something, and that there are instances when they also represent what is beyond the literal meaning. In the most literal sense, acceptance refers to the action of receiving something.

Old school mental health practitioners have promoted the idea of acceptance as learning how to live with something, and in this example, anxiety. However, this notion could be detrimental as it may build an internal conflict that can cause confusion and can even make the anxiety worse.

From the ACT perspective, acceptance and letting go means turning something into another object that can help you live a more meaningful life. This kind of thinking will not only empower you but will also undermine the power of anxiety. Much like anger, anxiety gets its strength from the way we respond to it. In the ATC context, acceptance means suspending all our judgment and becoming more conscious as if we are observing ourselves from the outside.

Letting go of anxiety can automatically happen when we stop judging and being afraid. If we are not aware of negative thoughts, we will end up fortifying our attachment to the things that could hurt us. It might seem that we are protecting ourselves by avoiding negative feelings, but sometimes, trying hard to eliminate something could result in an even stronger attachment.

Being Present

ACT encourages the persistent non-judgmental link between environmental and psychological events as they happen. The objective is for us to feel a more straightforward experience so that we increase the flexibility of our behavior and so our actions could be more aligned with the values that are important to us. We can achieve this by permitting our behavior to be influenced by our workability, and also through language to take note and describe events and not to merely judge or predict them.

A study conducted by Harvard University reveals that humans spend 50% of their time daydreaming. This is a surprising fact considering the limited time we have. Humans have the ability to detach from the present and think over the past or the future. This is considered as a gift because we can revisit our past and learn from it to improve ourselves. This will allow us to grow as individuals and as a society as we can collectively look after our wellbeing.

It also allows us to plan for our future. It is a good thing if we can anticipate what could happen in the next few years to come. Our ability to place ourselves in the possible situation will allow us to think how we can deal with different circumstances when they happen.

However, if our daydreaming can result in emotional disturbance, they could significantly affect our mental health and steal our happiness. It becomes a burden – a hurdle that we need to overcome.

Too much thinking about the past could lead us down the path of regrets or the inability to accept and let things go. It should not be altogether eliminated because it allows us to plan for the future. However, thinking too much of the future can be a bad thing because it could mean that we are not living our lives to the fullest and that we are wasting our time and energy preparing for scenarios that aren't even likely to happen.

Daniel Gilbert, a renowned psychologist from Harvard University, explores the psychological immune system that activates during stressful events allowing us to cope. More often than not, these things are not as bad as we had expected them to be. Overthinking about something is proven to be just a waste of time and resources.

Another study conducted by Harvard psychologist Dr. Matt Killingsworth reveals that humans are far less happy when they are daydreaming. Focusing on worries about the future can easily rob you the gift of the present. It could prevent you from actually doing something to improve your situation. Time is important and while daydreaming is not always a bad thing, spending too much time on it is not a good idea. That time could have been spent with family or friends. Spending too much time away from the present is not a good way to experience life.

It will take time and effort to teach our minds not to daydream too much, but it is doable. Here are some pointers you can follow:

Practice Mindfulness
You don't need to be a monk who is adept at meditation to practice the art of mindfulness. Try the mindfulness exercises in chapter 13.

You can practice the simple joy of being conscious and aware by making the effort to eat your breakfast without any form of distraction. Feel the warmth of coffee in your mouth, savor the bittersweet taste and smell the aroma of the wonderful drink. Try to use your five senses and what you can gain from the present. Try to do this as regularly as you can, but for starters, you can begin with a simple activity that you regularly do every day.

Regain the Focus on the Simplicity of Life
As soon as you notice that your mind is wandering off again, immediately regain your focus. Get your attention back to something that is simple and monotonous right at the moment. It could be a piece of paper, a paper bill, a cup of coffee, a notebook, or even just your hand.

Try to focus on things that will not trigger any emotion. The goal is to concentrate all of your attention on the item that will bring your awareness back to the present. You can do this each time you find yourself daydreaming until you are ready to naturally move on to what it is that you are actually doing.

Do New Things Every Day

Have you realized that when we were kids, the day seems to slowly pass by? This is partly because when we were kids, we are experiencing life for the first time, and processing it all requires our complete attention. It is ideal to focus our attention when we try new things and notice how much of the attention we manage to win over. We have to focus so we can learn how to do something. We generally have to steer ourselves to the present as we do or learn to do new things.

It can be fairly easy to give in to the habit of always looking forward. We usually do so in order to avoid a frustrating result – we want to be prepared for the worst case scenario, or stay on top of things. That's why we sometimes spend too much time with our minds wandering instead of enjoying the present. As a result, we sometimes fail to truly experience the precious moments of our life. It is great to have a plan, but it could be detrimental if we spend our time thinking about the thousands of possible scenarios that probably aren't going to ever happen.

Cognitive Defusion

ACT encourages us to defuse or detach ourselves from harmful thinking patterns through a core process known as cognitive defusion. The idea is that we all have the tendency to become too attached to our thoughts, and we tend to blow things out of proportion. Once we become too fused -- too much attached -- to our thoughts, they become stronger.

We need to accept the reality that thoughts are only thoughts. This statement is not designed to diminish the emotional effects of thoughts or to deny the reality that thoughts could help us be more aware of what is happening around us. These ideas are valid, but the point is that our thoughts are no stronger than we allow them to become. There are words and images that float through our mind, but we are the ones responsible for giving meaning to them.

It is not necessary to always respond to our ideas. When we think about something that is strong or frightening, there is usually a sense of urgency linked to them that could drive us to act immediately. If thoughts pop into your mind or if you have thoughts that you just can't shake off, it is best to apply the principles of acceptance and mindfulness before you take action.

Cognitive defusion is the practice of observing thoughts instead of becoming attached with the thought, looking at thoughts instead of looking from thoughts, and allowing thoughts to come by and then go instead of becoming attached to them.

Through cognitive defusion, we can observe the essence of our thoughts - that they are mere words or images that our mind conjures because of the emotions we feel. It will also help us respond to our thoughts by taking a workable action that is based on what actually works.

This is where mindfulness could also come in handy. We need to be able to recognize when we are too attached to thoughts. They should not always dictate our behavior.

Cognitive defusion is also effective if we need to change the thoughts that serve as obstacles in trying to live a life that is based on values.

Try assessing yourself about how you respond to your thoughts. But keep in mind that using cognitive defusion doesn't mean that thoughts are naturally harmful. Our capacity as humans to think and make sense of our thoughts allows us to live a more dynamic life.

Thinking patterns could become detrimental if they are causing considerable tension or stress. You may choose to start becoming more aware of your thoughts instead of becoming more attached with them. Their strength is only amplified by our illusion that these thoughts are stronger than us.

Self as Context

Because of relational frames such as Here vs. There, Now vs. Then, and I vs. You, the human language is directed to the context of self, and builds a spiritual, transcendent side our humanity.

This concept is one of the core tenets of RFT and ACT, and there is now a progressive evidence of its essence to the functions of language such as sense of self, theory of mind, and empathy.

Self as context is also crucial in ACT because it allows someone to be aware of his own flow of experience without forming any form of attachment. Self as context is developed in ACT through experiential processes, metaphors, and mindfulness exercises.

Mindfulness is the seed of this core process, as this will allow you to get in touch with your senses. This will harness your skill in observing yourself. For example, through this core process, you can take a closer look at your own human development and where you are in life. You will be aware of the influence of your upbringing and how it could affect your future.

Mindfulness is a critical aspect of ACT. That's why we have devoted a full chapter about it to help you understand this subject.

Values

In the context of cognitive behavior, values refer to specific qualities that warrant purposeful action.

In ACT, your specialist will encourage you to perform exercises that will help you select your direction in life in different areas such as career, family, and spirituality. This will also help you undermine the verbal processes that could lead to decisions that are based on attachment, social compliance, or avoidance.

For example, parents generally value honesty. A good person values integrity. A good leader values justice.

Remember, in the core processes of being present, defusion, and acceptance are not individual psychotherapy techniques but rather, they serve as guideposts for a more vital life that is consistent with the values that are important for you.

How to Discover Your Personal Core Values

Discovering your personal values will allow you to find the specific traits that reflect your needs, wants, and what you really care about life. By exploring your inner self to look for your core values, you can find great forces that will guide you in your decisions. This will also help you figure out what to seek and what to avoid. Through this core ACT process, you can start harnessing your own moral compass. Personal core values can serve as your guide posts on what you really cherish, and when you are in a difficult situation, you can choose to behave based on the standards you have set for yourself.

Step 1 - Be Conscious of Your Emerging Values
Mindfulness plays a crucial role in discovering your values. To do this, you should first find a quiet place where no one can disturb you. Exploring

your inner self to find your personal values require your own space and time. Turn off your phone, listen to calming music, or anything that can help you focus and relax. Some people use aromatherapy. Lavender oil is especially calming.

Step 2 - Remember Happy and Sad Moments in Your Life
Begin the process of discovering your personal values by writing down the moments that you have experienced great happiness or sadness. Try to remember the peaks and valleys of your experiences and take note of the details that surround every memory. Focus on the memories that had the most significant influence in your life instead of those where you have earned recognition or praise.

For example, you might have experienced great joy when your family visited a beach for the first time. This may not have been the best moment for your success, but this could be the root memory for your personality and how you bond with your loved ones.

Explore the common themes that run through your strongest memories, which could be influenced by your religious beliefs or political affiliation. There's a good chance that you will find specific things that will trigger strong emotions of anger, sadness, injustice, or a combination of these things. Take note of the things that are missing and then try to look for value during your most joyous moments.

Step 3 - Examine Human Needs in General
We all have our basic needs based on the composition of our bodies and our common needs within the society we belong to. Our personal values generally stem from our needs. Hence, we feel strong passion and commitment towards our values. By exploring human needs, we can gain a powerful boost to define our personal values. Basically, the universal needs of humans include:

- Physical (food, water, shelter, clothes)
- Peace (hope, acceptance, ease of mind)
- Connection (consideration, respect, warmth)
- Autonomy (self-expression, dignity, choice)
- Play (joy, humor, adventure)
- Meaning (understanding, participation, celebration)

Step 4 – Create A Draft of Your Personal Core Values

Make a temporary list of the personal core values you believe you cannot live without. In this step, you have to connect your personal experiences with the values that are important in your culture (and to you) on top of the fundamental needs of humans based on our biological composition.

Write the values that using wording that holds true for yourself. For example, if you value truth, you may want to write this as "I value the courage of honesty and integrity."

Try to start with at least seven core values, but take note that this could be trimmed down to at least three core values later on in the process.

Step 5 - Write About How You Usually Practice These Values

Personal values could be different from the strategies you use to define them. More often than not, these strategies are based on the values of your family. By understanding how you practice your personal values, you can gain better insight into the values that influence you to do things that you can be proud of.

For example, you may choose service as one of your personal core values. Will you practice this value by running for an elected position or by volunteering in a charitable organization? If you value peace, do you discourage noise in your home, or are you more active in seeking reconciliation between people who disagree with each other? It is crucial to make these strong connections between your values and the things that you tend to do every day.

Step 6 - Look at the Results of Your Decisions
You can do this step in either imagined or real situations that require decisions. How will you decide if you value love of family, and you have to pick between staying with your loved ones and pursuing a career overseas? If you value independence, and you are given a choice to move in with your special someone, will you do it?

In these scenarios, your personal values could really help you in making creative decisions that mirror how you care for yourself and the people around you. You should understand that you can see the value in action when you need to make a real-life decision. There are times that we are so attached to a certain core value that we always think it will result in the best decision.

Step 7 - Make the Final List of Your Personal Core Values
By doing the first six steps, you should be able to make the final lists of values that you really care about. Remember, these values must be based on your initial inclination on what is essential for you. Moreover, you should integrate what you learned about writing down your values and testing them out in different scenarios. Try to trim down three to four primary values.

These values are effective tools. Personal core values can reshape your brain to live the life you really want.

Committed Action
After defining your personal core values that you want to be central in your life, you now need to use these values to guide a list of actions you need to take. Even though it is crucial to gain knowledge of your personal

core values, it will be a waste of time if you don't act on these values to live by. You should start to make the conscious choice as well as the commitment to practice every value you hold dear through your actions.

Committed action could mean engaging in general patterns of effective actions, which are influenced by your personal core values. Flexibility and adaptability are crucial for the committed action to be effective. This will allow you to easily adapt to any change in your life without compromising your values.

But regardless of how many lapses you commit, you should never give up. You need to review your actions and have them aligned with your values.

By gaining a deeper understanding of your values, you can start setting goals for your life that are based on these values. For instance, if you value hard work, a solid goal can help you become more productive and efficient in the workplace. Your goals in life will definitely change as the needs arise, while values should be consistent and should be used as your motivational boost in guiding how you behave.

In the ACT context, committed action has four steps:

1. Select a specific aspect of your life that you really want to change
2. Select the personal core values you like to pursue in this area in your life
3. Establish goals that are based on your values
4. Mindfully take the necessary actions

The bigger objective of transforming values into committed action is to live a life that is filled with purpose, which is guided by the values that are important to you. If you think that your life is going nowhere or out of balance, it is possible that these feelings are caused by not acting based on your values or being out of touch with your core values. When you become mindful of your actions, you can start to take the needed steps to transform these values into committed action.

The ACT Process for Setting Up Goals

ACT encourages setting up of goals that are based on values. It specifies three major steps:

Step 1 - Choose an area in your life that you want to work on.

This may include community, romance, education, career, personal growth, environment, family, parenting, health, finances, and many more.

Step 2 - Establish goals that are SMART - Specific, Meaningful, Adaptive, Realistic, and Time-Bound.

Specific - Try to be specific as possible on what actions you want to take. Be sure that you are aware of the involved steps in taking the necessary action. A specific goal is easier to achieve compared to a general goal. For example, just setting up the goal of spending more time with your child may not allow you to know if you have already achieved it. A more specific goal is to spend at least one-hour playtime every day. Being specific with your goal will allow you to assess whether you have already accomplished the goal or not and monitor your progress.

Meaningful - Assess if your goal is genuinely based on your values in comparison with a strict rule or a sense of what you must do. If you think that your goals don't have a deeper sense of purpose or meaning, try to assess if the goal is really influenced by the values you hold dear. Take note that your core values should be based on things that provide meaning to your life.

Adaptive - Make sure that your goal will help you follow a direction that you think will greatly improve your life. Assess if your goal will move you closer or is steering you away from the real purpose of your life.

Realistic - There's a big chance that you will only feel disappointment, frustration, or failure if you have set goals that are not really attainable. You should try to find a balance between setting goals that are quite easy versus goals that are impossible to achieve. Be realistic and practical if you can really push yourself to achieve your goals.

Time-Bound - You can specify your goals even more by adding a time and date by which you want to accomplish the goal. If this is not possible, or not realistic, try setting up a time frame and do everything you can to make certain that you work within this bond.

Step 3 - Define the Urgency of Your Goals
The last step is to define the urgency that your goal should be accomplished. Your goals could be:

- Long-term - Create a plan of the necessary actions you need to take so you can be closer to your goals over the span of six months to one year.
- Medium-term - Think about the necessary actions you need to take so you can move towards your goals within two to three months
- Short-term goals - Make a list of the things you need to do so you can achieve your goals within a month
- Immediate goal - What are the goals that you need to achieve within a week or even within the day?

Starting to live in accordance with your personal core values will fan the flames of your committed action.

Our best plan and values will not be meaningful if they are not supported by action. Equipped with the knowledge of the core values you really want to pursue, you can start moving forward towards living a valuable life.

Conclusion

Thank you and congratulations for making it to this part of the book. I hope you have learned a lot about different forms and techniques of behavioral therapy, and you are now better armed to reshape your life. By now, you should have a better understanding of the possible treatment program you want to try.

Which specific psychotherapy techniques have caught your attention? Are you into the goal-based CBT? Or perhaps you want to try practicing mindfulness exercise under ACT? You may choose to work alone and personalize your approach, but during the initial stages, it is ideal to work with a professional therapist who will serve as your partner in this journey towards living a life with meaning.

Continue your exploration of behavioral therapies, and try to do the following tips as part of the next steps:

1. Choose top 3 specific techniques you want to try. Read more about them, and try to seek an appointment with professionals who are specializing in these techniques.
2. Join online forums, subscribe to blogs, or seek membership with local clubs or organizations that will help you to immerse more with helpful techniques.
3. Reach out to people suffering from the same condition as you are and try to help them. The advantage of being empowered is that you can also share all the things you have gained - knowledge, skills, and attitude.

Please do not let this book be the end of your learning experience and the pursuit of self-empowerment. Keep in mind that the psychotherapy community is gearing for more research and in improving the treatment programs to help more people.

Your part is to lookout for these developments so you can continue to grow and reshape your life and the lives of people you care about.

Made in the USA
Columbia, SC
02 March 2021